The Petigru Review

2015

I0538296

Volume 9

The Petigru Review — 2015
Volume 9

ISBN-13: 978-0971461871

ISBN-10: 0971461872

The Petigru Review • 2015 • Volume 9
© 2015 by the South Carolina Writers' Workshop.
All rights reserved.

Printed and bound in the United States of America.

Published with support from the
South Carolina Arts Commission by:

South Carolina Writers' Workshop
4711 Forest Drive, Suite 3, PMB 189
Columbia, SC 29206

Photo by Barbara V. Evers

This project is funded in part by the Cultural Council of Richland and Lexington Counties and the South Carolina Arts Commission, which receives support from the National Endowment for the Arts and the John and Susan Bennett Memorial Arts Fund of the Coastal Community Foundation of SC.

Also sponsored by:
Fiction Addiction
1020A Woodruff Road
Greenville SC 29607
864.675.0540
www.fiction-addiction.com

Contents

THE PETIGRU REVIEW

Fiction

Creative Nonfiction

Contributors

Photo Credits

TPR Judges

From the Editor

IN 2010 I JOINED SCWW and volunteered to be on the Board of Directors. Everyone on the Board has a job, large or small. As a newbie I volunteered to take over *The Petigru Review*.

I was a neophyte who knew nothing about editing, let alone typography and publishing. I learned, and, I hope, have shepherded five good issues of this anthology to press, plus this one.

Along the way I've seen stories and poems expressing the positive aspects of the human condition with eloquence, wit and grace. Along the way we've published pieces that exemplify the worst of the human condition, sometimes with humor, sometimes with chilling realism.

I've seen authors' joy at their first publication and seasoned authors thrilled to be published in our pages. The rewards are amazing. I've met writers and other editors whose support has been heartwarming.

Having been on the Board of Directors for six years, the past two as President, I must step down for a year. So I managed to inveigle Irena Tervo as the next editor, and an editorial assistant, Elaine Holladay.

We also administer the Carrie McCray Memorial Literary Awards.

In April, at the busiest time for *TPR*, I had a partial knee replacement. It simply could not wait any longer. While I was recuperating, Irena and Elaine took over. Elaine recruited the judges and gathered the manuscripts. She sent them to the judges, and she and Irena collated the results. We made editorial notes on the chosen manuscripts and passed them around, each adding comments.

In preparation for taking over next year as editor Irena put together the initial draft of the book. She did an amazing job. All that was left were the tweaks. I'm leaving *The Petigru Review* in capable hands.

Trilby Plants

From the Assistant Editor

THE BOAT ON THE FRONT COVER of this edition of *The Petigru Review* reminds me of Hemingway's *The Old Man and the Sea*, about an unlucky fisherman named Santiago who goes out in a small boat and spends two days and nights battling hunger, the elements and man-eating sharks while pursuing a giant marlin – the catch of his lifetime. Santiago's struggle reminds me of the writing process.

Writers cast their ideas into the waters of their imagination. They wait in that boat, alternating patience and frenzied work. Sometimes there is success, but often there is just a rod in the water. Like fishermen, writers can't always predict what happens beneath the sea. The process can be a mystery, other times it is mystical.

To the Carrie McCray winners and published authors in TPR, I am honored to be a part of this wonderful 'catch' in an abundant season. I congratulate Trilby for bringing TPR to a new level in the six years she has been the editor, and to extend a heartfelt thanks to the SCWW board for entrusting it to me next year.

And to all authors everywhere, being a writer is not just about the catch. Perhaps the most important thing is getting into that little skiff and rowing out to sea.

Irena Tervo

Winners
Carrie McCray Memorial
Literary Awards

FIRST CHAPTER OF A NOVEL

The Dark Side of Town

Sasscer Hill

DENSE FOG ENVELOPED the backstretch at Saratoga Race Course that morning, leaving the Oklahoma training track virtually invisible. Still, I could smell its sandy dirt and sense the expanse of the mile oval stretching away from me. Jogging the gravel path that paralleled the track, I shoved my hands deeper into the pockets of my jacket, hugging the black denim tighter around my rib cage against the dawn chill.

Out on the dirt the pounding of hooves drew closer, the sound muffled in the moisture-laden air. Beyond the rail, the horses flying past me were ill-defined, almost ghostly.

The sudden, deafening crack of a handgun was neither muffled nor poorly defined. My years as a Baltimore street cop left no doubt what I heard. I stood still, eyes and ears straining.

Ahead, someone screamed, "Oh, my God."

I raced forward. The high-pitched wails of a woman grew louder. As I drew close, I could make out her thin figure, her pale face staring at a form splayed on the ground at her feet. The acrid scent of gunpowder floated past me. The coppery stench of blood was unmistakable.

I closed the distance between us. "Hey," I said, heading off her next cry. "Maybe you should step back. Cops will come. You don't want to mess up the scene, right?"

Though she'd stopped screaming, she didn't seem to hear me. She stared at the figure on the ground, her body shaking. I stared, too. Male, the back of his head blown out, his hand still clutching a revolver. Suicide?

The woman moaned. I could almost see another scream rising in her throat. "Do you have a phone?" I said, trying to distract her. "Hey, look at me." She did, her eyes huge and round. "Do you know him?"

"I, no. I mean, I've seen him before. At the track."

Gently, I grasped her arm. "Come on. Don't stare at him anymore. We need to get help. Do you have a phone?" I said again.

She nodded numbly.

"Okay, good. Call 911."

I had almost pulled my cell to make the call, before stopping. Though no longer a street cop, I was working undercover and needed to keep a low profile.

When the woman talked to the dispatcher, she grew more focused, giving her name, saying a man had been shot– or maybe shot himself– at the Oklahoma training track just inside the East Avenue entrance to Saratoga's backstretch.

"No," she said, "I ran over here when I heard the gun go off, and I saw – "

The dispatcher must have sensed her building hysteria and said something to divert it. As they are trained to do, he kept his witness on the phone.

The mist began to break up and rose toward the treetops and spires crowning the historic wooden barns to my right. I eased away from the woman, stepped into a lingering column of fog and glanced back. Good, I could barely see her. I shouldn't be involved in this shooting. I double-timed it toward my original destination, the barn where I worked as a hot walker.

In the distance, a police siren wailed. The sound drew closer as I hurried away.

Later that morning, I led a hot, sweaty racehorse named Bionic along my barn's dusty aisle and listened for gossip about the shooting everyone said was a suicide. The guy had apparently been an apprentice jockey from

South America, only no one knew much about him. They said he'd just arrived from Ecuador, or Chile, or maybe Uruguay.

"Whoa back," I called to Becky Joe, the groom who led her horse behind me.

I stopped Bionic to allow him a few sips of water, and as he sank his lips into the bucket hanging from the shedrow rail, I rolled back his cooler sheet to see if his reddish brown coat was drying out. Thirsty, he sucked up the water until I pulled him away. He was still too hot to drink much, and I rolled the sheet back over his neck so the cool air hitting his wet coat wouldn't cause muscle cramping.

I glanced back at Becky Joe Benson. Maybe sixty, she was short, wore high-heeled cowboy boots and a brown suede Stetson years past its glory days. I turned back and headed down the shedrow with Becky Joe behind. At this track, the two of us were nobodies, yet we led a couple of horses worth hundreds of thousands of dollars.

I'd been on the job at this barn a week and hadn't figured Becky out yet. She had a drinking problem, used to be a jockey, then an unsuccessful trainer, and had fallen down the ranks to groom. But she was smart and unquestionably well educated. No doubt she had a story. Everyone at the racetrack did.

Her filly was farther along in the cooling process than my colt. She was dried out enough that Becky had already removed her sheet. When I glanced back, Becky let the filly empty her water bucket, then led the horse into a stall to see if she wanted to pee.

I walked on, passing equine heads that peered over stall gates or snatched bites of hay from the nets fastened outside their stalls. The sharp tang of liniment stung my nose, and somewhere, a metal-shod hoof struck the inside of one of the stalls which had been there since 1863. Many legends had raced at Saratoga.

I tried to concentrate on these things, but my mind wanted to play games with me, flitting back to the acrid odor of burnt gunpowder and the metallic reek of blood. The image of the jockey's blown out head, the terrible smell of death. What darkness had made him give up on life?

I turned the corner at the end of the aisle and was so lost in my thoughts, I almost ran into Stevie Davis. Skinny and young, Stevie might reach five-foot-three– if his socks were thick enough. During the few days I'd worked at Saratoga, the gaunt lines on the kid's face seemed to have increased. It made no sense to me. His frame was so scrawny, he didn't need to starve himself to make jockey weight. Something else was eating him.

Catching my eye, the seventeen-year-old did an about-face and walked alongside me and Bionic. "Fay," he said, "you hear about that guy that shot himself?"

I almost corrected him, since my real name is Fia McKee. But at Saratoga Race Course that summer I needed people to believe I was Fay Mason. Using aliases for undercover work in the past, I'd found it safer to stick with my own initials.

"It's all I've heard all morning," I said. "Why do you think he did it?"

"I don't know. Whole thing creeps me out." But his lips curved upward, and the troubled look in his eyes receded a moment as he smiled at me. He was a good-looking kid, with light brown hair, clear, intelligent eyes, and a honed face with good bones. Still, he carried worry lines that shouldn't be there. Stevie was the stable jockey for the Saratoga trainer I'd been sent to investigate, a thug named Marzio (aka Mars) Pizutti.

As we walked on, I could smell Bionic's sweat, hear the breath blowing from his nostrils, and see where the flesh immediately above his eye was slightly sunken with exhaustion. His reddish-brown coat was offset by jet black legs, mane, and tail, the classic markings of a blood bay.

"He doing okay?" Stevie said, staring at the horse. "He's supposed to race in a few weeks, and I'll get the call."

"Pizutti knows more about that than me," I said.

Stevie had just worked the colt five-eighths of a mile, and Bionic's cardiovascular system was not recovering as quickly as Pizutti probably wanted. Personally, I thought the horse would have been better off working three-eighths with a gallop out at whatever speed he was comfortable with. But as a lowly hot walker, my opinion was irrelevant.

At the end of the shedrow, Pizutti – cocky, rotund, and egotistical – emerged from his office.

I thought I heard Stevie say, "Oh shit," under his breath, but couldn't swear to it. As much as I disliked what I knew about Pizutti, I had to admit he had an uncanny connection with his horses. He had a soft round face, was a little jowly beneath his chin, and his expression, as usual, was bland, making me wonder what it was about the man that made Stevie so uncomfortable. Pizutti glanced at Bionic, then flicked his gaze over me.

"Hey, what's your name again?"

Photo from Pixabay - CCO Public Domain

"Fay," I said.

"Yeah, right. Let me see that horse."

"Yes, sir." You'd think the guy would know his horse's name. I hadn't spoken to him much in the few days I'd been there. Mostly he'd fired instructions and I'd nodded and gotten on with it.

I led the big colt to him and stopped. Stevie edged away and stood against the wall as Pizutti placed his palm on Bionic's chest to see how much dampness and heat remained.

Pizutti glanced at me. "I tell you what, Fay. It's kinda like a fine line, you know? Too much or too little. I think he maybe did too much today." He pursed his lips as if annoyed with himself. "Keep him going."

"Yes sir." I smelled stale beer on him.

"Hey," he said, "I keep telling you. Lose the 'sir' stuff. Call me 'Mars.' Right?"

His voice held a whining quality, the volume always soft, like maybe he'd been unhappy as a kid and hadn't wanted to draw attention.

"Okay, Mars," I said.

I clucked to Bionic and moved forward. Stevie started to follow.

"Hey," Mars said, crooking a finger at the kid. "Wait up. Need to talk to you 'bout something."

The jockey paused, and I headed down the shedrow with Bionic, thinking how my work for the Thoroughbred Racing Protection Bureau (TRPB), sometimes placed me in risky situations. I believed in the agency's mission to protect the integrity of horse racing, but with the immense sums of money involved and the cash that poured into online betting outlets, we fought an uphill battle. The lowlifes that would do anything for money were never far away.

This big picture didn't affect me emotionally. A jockey eating his gun did. And smaller things struck a heartstring, too. Like the haunted eyes of Stevie Davis, or the game-on face of a racehorse determined to annihilate his competitors. The exalted, shouting bettor trading high fives with his buddies because he'd won, or the slumped shoulders and frightened face of a man who just bet borrowed money and lost. That stuff touches my soul.

Bionic snorted as a calico stable cat darted across the aisle in front of the colt's hooves. The horse stopped, lowered his head and blew gently on the cat. She arched her back and bumped it against the horse's nose before streaking into a stall.

I clucked to my horse, we moved on and I considered my personal goal – to protect the people and animals that make racing such a phenomenal sport. And they needed protecting from Mars Pizutti.

The guy was backed by powerful people, and his horses won a lot of races. Too many races. He'd had numerous infractions and suspensions. He'd filed false times for works and managed to place fictional ones in the *Daily Racing Form*. He used body building anabolic steroids like Stanozolol and anti-inflammatory corticosteroids like Prednisone. Though these were allowed, they could be administered no closer than thirty days before a race, and Pizutti had trouble keeping his dates straight. Yet, he'd always gotten off with a fine and been back in his barn within days.

The New York Racing Association had finally suffered enough and had solicited the TRPB to plant an agent in Pizutti's barn. As a hot walker, I was almost invisible as I led horses each morning, able to watch, listen, record and photograph the goings on in the trainer's barn.

By now, Bionic and I had walked past the long row of stalls on the rear side of the barn and turned the corner back to Pizutti's shedrow. The trainer was talking to Stevie at the far end of the aisle. The jockey had his arms crossed over his chest, and though I was still thirty stalls away, his stance appeared defensive.

Since Bionic had been the last horse out on the course that day, it was late in the morning. Much of the help had finished up and headed to the track kitchen for lunch, leaving the barn quiet, the morning bustle noticeably subdued.

Two stalls down, Becky Joe stepped onto the shedrow holding a tote stuffed with grooming tools, hoof picks, a bottle of liniment, and rolls of Vetrap. Her other hand held a tub of poultice. Apparently, she'd just finished "doing up" her filly's legs.

As she stopped and waited for me to go by, I heard raised voices. A quick look ahead showed Stevie shaking his head no.

"Been in that boy's shoes," Becky Joe muttered. "Didn't like it then, don't like seeing it now."

"What's going on?" I said.

She stared at her scuffed leather boots. "Couldn't say."

I walked on, growing close enough to hear Stevie's next words.

"I won't do it."

"You God damn will."

"No I – "

"Shut up," Mars said. He'd seen me coming. Whatever they were arguing about, he didn't want me hearing it.

An angry shade of red stained Stevie's cheeks. The worry lines around his eyes were starting to look like canyons.

The image of the dead apprentice jockey was freshly stamped in my brain, and now I saw desperation in Stevie's eyes. Like Becky Joe, I didn't like it.

Photo by Irena Tervo

Photo Courtesy Isabel J. Kurek Photography

SASSCER HILL, a former Maryland racehorse breeder, trainer and rider, uses the sport of kings as a backdrop for her mysteries. Her "vivid descriptive" prose about greed, evil, heart and courage propelled her novels to multiple award nominations including an Agatha, a Macavity and the Dr. Tony Ryan Best in Racing Literature Award. Hill earned a BA in English Literature from Franklin and Marshall College and now lives with her husband in Aiken, SC.

SasscerHill.com

Shakespeare's Daughters

S. Jane Gari

LENA WAS HAVING A GIRL. A little girl with cysts on her brain. Dr. Linden wanted to do more tests. Tests. The word consumed the air in the room, making the thin gown draping Lena's body grate against her skin.

Her husband, Christian, couldn't get the day off.

"No big deal," she'd told him.

But it was. The twenty-week ultrasound revealed the baby's gender, and for the Carmichael's baby, it also revealed a problem.

Everything in the examination room was too bright. She blinked against the fluorescent lights, and once she started she couldn't stop. The doctor thumbed some papers in a manila folder while her mouth moved.

> "Trisomy-18....*"a serious genetic defect that causes mental retardation and multiple organ system failures...."*

But Lena heard nothing except an almost electrical humming in her ears. The baby rolled against in her belly – a curious fluttering sensation that almost tickled. Lena stroked the place on her belly where she'd sensed contact.

She felt herself coming to the surface now, studying the kind face of the doctor who was only trying to tell her what she needed to know. The world unmuted itself, and Lena forced herself to listen to the words.

Dr. Linden's slight frame belied the power with which she punctured the silence. "The cysts and lack of expected growth and development at this stage in the pregnancy lead us to believe that the baby may have Trisomy-18." She pulled something from the folder, and Lena accepted the cold, flat grenade disguised as a pamphlet.

The words blurred beyond a gauzy scrim of tears: "...*a serious genetic defect that causes mental retardation and multiple organ system failures....*"

"We may be wrong, Lena. And I hope to God we are. But when two or more indicators are there for the syndrome, we need to take a closer look." The doctor held one of Lena's shaking hands. "We'll need to do more ultrasounds, amniocentesis. Run some blood work. If the test results are positive for Trisomy-18 then we can discuss your options...."

Lena struggled to breathe normally and watched the baby suck her thumb on the ultrasound monitor. Lena was already in love with her.

"Options? Are you suggesting...I can't terminate...I won't." Lena let the doctor hold her hand and rub circles over the peaks and valleys of her white knuckles.

"Let's get more information first, so you have all the facts. Ultimately, you and your husband will decide what's right for your family."

Lena did not remember the drive home on the Long Island Expressway and drifted up the hardwood stairs of her Cape Cod to the newly-decorated nursery. Mint-green walls and plush, yellow crib bedding. For a moment, Lena wished she were tiny enough to dissolve into the coziness of this room populated by pastel animals – wished she were a child herself. She longed for her parents, but her usual mental armor defended her against letting those thoughts unfold.

Lena scanned the menagerie of soft critters that peered out from the shelves and pulled one down: a blue bear the size of her own torso. She hugged the bear, pressed it to her petite frame, and settled into a rocking chair next to the shelves. Seeing her own ripe belly swelling beneath her dress had been amazing to her only yesterday. But now she was pinned to a chair by her worry, nearly strangling a stuffed animal to keep from screaming.

She wanted to erase this last ultrasound, to daydream about what the child would look like. Would she have Lena's dark brown hair with its odd cowlick at the crown, her hazel eyes and freckled skin? Or would she favor Christian? His eyes like Indian turquoise, black hair and ruddy skin.

Lena rocked manically in the chair that had been her great-grandmother's, as if doing so could transport her, or at the very least induce a Zen-like forgetfulness, however fleeting.

She focused on the movement of the rocking chair, digging into the cream carpet with a light swooshing that sounded like a heartbeat – a baby's heartbeat that Lena swore she felt fluttering beneath the cotton of her dress. She would be the third generation to rock a child in this chair. She hoped.

Her uncertainty guided her to the spare room they used as an office, egging her on to conduct research on Trisomy-18. Christian always liked the soft electric crackling of the computer when it came alive. Now, to Lena, the low pops and hisses sounded like the lit fuse of a bomb. But she had to know what they might be up against. Might – she cradled the word in her mind as she typed, *Trisomy-18*.

A few hours later, Lena sat in the kitchen for a late dinner with Christian. Dark cherry cabinets insulated the walls and softened the shock of garish potholders that dangled from hooks on either side of the black stove. The potholders had been crocheted by her mother. Christian thought they were tacky. They usually made Lena smile, but not tonight. The couple pushed food around on their plates for thirty minutes while snow fell on the half-frozen pond outside. The sonogram image from the ultrasound bore witness at the head of the table.

"I'm sorry I couldn't get someone to cover my classes today. I should have been there for you," he said.

"It's okay. The new semester just started. Stony Brook wouldn't be thrilled if you left organic chemistry in the hands of an undergrad assistant. Not yours anyway. He's a complete flake. There's nothing we can do anyway. Just wait it out. Hope for the best."

"We don't have to just wait. We should do the testing at the specialty clinic that Dr. Linden recommended."

"I don't want to go to the specialty clinic. You know what the sign says on their door? 'High-Risk Pregnancy.' Makes me feel like I have a disease. Pregnancy is not a disease."

"But Trisomy-18 is," said Christian.

He was in lecture-mode. She could feel it. Her toes clenched and unclenched deep in her shoes.

"You just read the same articles I did," he said. "We're looking at the cysts on this sonogram. If the fetus tests positive, do you really want to do this? More than half of them die during the third trimester. Ninety-five percent of those that do survive, die before they're one. Ninety-five percent. Multiple organ system disorders, mental retardation. You want to risk that?"

"The 'fetus?' Just yesterday you said 'baby.' We said, 'maybe Alys,' even though you want to spell it A-l-i-c-e." Lena stopped to read his face — lips stretched in a line, head bent to the side. Waiting-for-acquiescence posture, but without the usual slight smile. "Stop being a scientist for a second and think like the father you're about to be."

"I am. I think we should get as much information as we can and then make a decision."

Snow gathered in the corners of the panes in their bay window, the white clumping against the black sky. She could feel herself sweating despite the draft the windows always let in.

"This isn't one of your chemistry classes," she said. "This is our baby. We picked out a name. I don't want a six-inch needle poking into her, a needle that might damage a perfectly healthy baby. There's a fifty percent chance that nothing is wrong at all. The cysts on her brain could go away on their own."

"Which means there's a fifty percent chance the fetus suffers from a catastrophic birth defect. Catastrophic. Lena, please. Think about that. Everyone will suffer. The... the baby. Us."

Her chest heaved. Christian grasped Lena's hands across the dark wood of the table as if he believed his grip could steady the reeling of their world.

He broke the silence. "I know you're attached to the baby already, in a way that I'm not going to pretend to understand. We don't have to decide one way or another right this second. We have a little time to work with. We'll figure it out."

Lena nodded, pursing her lips together. "I'm sorry I'm challenging you on this. I have the same fears you do, about how difficult it would be if the baby's that sick. But I saw her. I saw her sucking her thumb on that screen, like a normal baby. What the doctors are saying *might* be wrong with her? I just don't want it to be true. I have to believe that it won't be true." Christian pulled her to her feet. They stood holding each other, swaying on the white tiles of their dimly-lit kitchen, feeling the whisper of the winter draft that moved the lace curtains. She let herself lean into him, his arms keeping her upright in the cocoon of his wool sweater infused with his warmth and the smell of his cologne: Sandalwood.

"Let's go upstairs," he said. "I'm exhausted. I still have to shower."

Lena was reluctant to leave the shelter of his arms. She felt like a refugee from her own life. "You go on up," she said. "I'll be up in a minute. I'm going to grab a cup of tea."

"Let me get it." Christian filled up a kettle and put it on the stove, then reached into the cabinet for a cup and the box of herbal teas. The minutia of such acts added up to one measureless sum. The chill in the room made her think of their even more drafty walk-up apartment in Port Jefferson and the morning after he'd asked her to marry him. She'd stuck her head out the window to gauge the temperature of the winter air. Christian had laughed and dragged her back into the room, asking her if she was trying to catch pneumonia while wrapping her in a blanket. He loved her. She loved him. She hoped it would be enough to navigate the coming months.

Christian's eyes focused on the stovetop, his long bangs clinging to the condensation gathering at his temples as the steam rose in plumes from the screaming kettle. It had taken them both a few beats to even hear the sound.

"There you go." He handed her the steeping tea.

"Thank you."

He leaned in to kiss her and then slid upstairs like a sleepwalker.

Lena sat alone at the kitchen table. The clock's ticking was relentless in the silence, like a dog you can't stop from barking. She used to be able to quiet her mind no matter how loud the distraction. That seemed a life-time ago. Lena thought of her mother teaching her how to meditate as a little girl. The quiet and intense focus. Could she remember how? She tried to focus on her breathing, but the tick-tick of the second hand still barked at her, derailed her thinking.

Lena hadn't believed in God for a long time. The Lord's Prayer tumbled through her brain in her father's voice. She clutched the half-globe of her cup, sending ripples across the tea's surface. "Please, God," she sobbed.

The sonogram fluttered, then drifted off the table to the floor. Bending over made her light-headed these days. With reluctance, Lena leaned over from her chair to pick up the picture.

And then she heard them, the strange noises that always preceded their arrival. She sat up straight, her pulse quickening.

"No," she said. The word hung solitary in the changing air.

An oven-sized cloud of lights hovered a mere five feet in front of her. They flurried in the center of the kitchen like a miniature flock of iridescent birds, or swarming fireflies. A vaguely electric hum inhabited the air, as if all the appliances were gearing up after a power surge. And a rush of whispering voices all saying the same thing – the words almost intelligible. Lena sat immobilized for a full five minutes, staring at them,

Photo © 2010 Mary Vican Flickr CCO Public Domain

studying the glow they cast on the metallic surfaces of the kitchen that amplified their iridescence the way glass ornaments bounce light around a Christmas tree.

The lights floated in front of her, unified in their movements as if magnetized. And then they twisted themselves into deliberate lines, taking shape, almost like a pentacle suspended in the air. Her fingers twitched. She thought about lifting her right hand, in salutation or defense. Just as she decided to be afraid, the lights swirled around the center of their swarm. As mysteriously as they had arrived, they disappeared, sucked into a tiny rip in the air itself.

They had reawakened. These glowing firefly-like beings had come back. For the past year, Lena had convinced herself they'd been illusions – a strange byproduct of her relationship with Justin. Making Justin the culprit had been enough to make them dormant. So why would they come to her now? Did they want something? Once again, the mystical imposed itself, threatening to crack the more grounded and normal world she thought she wanted. That she did want.

"Christian."

Still in the shower. She thought about screaming for him again, but what good would come of that? She already knew she would keep the real root of her anxiety from Christian – the lights were connected to Justin, and their arrival meant something even if she didn't know what. If she worked up the nerve to tell him, he would probably analyze the phenomenon to death, take the magic out of it. He'd derive a hypothesis involving possible angles of light in the kitchen at that time of night and the biological stress of pregnancy. Besides, she couldn't explain the whole story of the firefly-things without explaining Justin.

She rubbed her temples, as if doing so could stop the reel of film in her mind's eye. Scenes of Justin's face. His impossible green eyes. Justin. The "fireflies." Her baby girl moving inside her. The doctor's words: "The cysts and lack of expected growth and development…Trisomy-18…"

The air in the kitchen seemed thin. She felt her body bracing for the sobs she could feel gathering in her chest, her throat. And then she let them come.

Christian knelt beside Lena on the kitchen floor where she had let herself fall apart.

She had overestimated how long he would be in the shower. His presence beside her hadn't even registered right away. He'd seen her crying and holding her head. Her body tensed as she searched her mind for an excuse, a reason she would be lying in a pile on the floor. A half-truth was always best.

"I'm just tired," she managed.

"What is it? Do you have a headache? I think we should go to the hospital." He wasn't asking. Keys were already jangling. The garage door was going up. The coat closet was opening.

White dashes dissolved beneath the Toyota as they sped toward Stony Brook Medical Center.

"My head doesn't even hurt. I'm just feeling a little overwhelmed. That's all." Lena still hadn't given up trying to get him to turn the car around.

"Better to be safe than sorry. You might be stressed out from the bad news today. But there could be something else going on."

Yes, there is. Small electric harbingers of who knows what popped into the kitchen for a visit. But how could she say that?

At the hospital, all of Lena's vital signs were normal. Another ultrasound. The baby's heart still fluttered, and the cysts still marred her unborn brain.

Three hours later, Lena felt Christian's chest inflating and deflating against her back as they spooned in their four-poster bed. The blood clicked through her veins, keeping her awake. She thought about her parents again, and breathing. In. Out. On the edge of sleep, she thought about the lights. Firefly lights. In their kitchen. In January. She built a closet in her mind, stuffed the lights in the corner and closed the door. It was an old trick for her by now.

S. JANE GARI is a three-time Pushcart Prize Nominee and award-winning author. She lives in Elgin, South Carolina with her husband and daughter. Jane is a firm believer that balance brings sanity. While writing an emotional abuse book (*Losing the Dollhouse*) that recounts real-life family drama and betrayal, she made time to pen some light-hearted potty humor (*Flush This Book*). Without a good laugh now and then, we'd all need to be institutionalized. When she's not writing, she's editing other people's work and tutoring children.

Photo by Valerie Keiser Norris

Faith, Hope, and Dr. Vangelis

Steve Gordy

IT WAS A BAD SIGN when Katie Lyle's oncologist ran late for an appointment.

The longer she waited, the more the dread welled inside her. When the delay stretched to forty-five minutes, her husband Andy started fuming. "Does he have any idea of what it would cost me if I kept a customer waiting this long?"

Katie kept her face placid, but her voice held a slight tremble. "I think I know why he's late." Her eyes misted.

Before her husband could reply, the office door opened. Doctors Eric Grueneberg and Clark Burton entered, murmuring quick apologies before they took seats facing the Lyles at a mahogany conference table.

Burton's presence was an unexpected and unwelcome surprise.

"Hello, Clark." Katie's voice wavered. "It was kind of you to come all the way from Tampa."

Burton's pate glistened beneath the fluorescent lights' chilly glow. He looked up from a red folder, his brow an array of deep furrows. Before he could speak, Eric said, "Clark just wants to be here to give you what assurance he can." His soft voice muffled the slight German accent in his speech.

She looked at him. "Just tell us what you know, whatever it is."

With a swift nod, Clark said, "All right. The latest imaging shows new lesions on your kidneys. An additional round of chemotherapy *might* slow down the growth rate, but – "

"But not stop it." Katie's calmness was natural, unforced.

Eric nodded. "It's really bad when it shows up in a solid organ. Remember that with chemotherapy, we have to balance how well it works with the damage it does to your body. You're pretty weak from all the rounds you've done so far."

She dabbed briefly at her eyes. "How long do I have?"

Eric glanced at Clark, who said, "Predictions are nothing but speculation. Anything I tell you would be a guess."

"So give me your best guess."

"Six weeks, perhaps."

Her sigh was almost inaudible. "I'll be dead before Christmas." Clark said nothing in reply. The resigned look in his eyes was answer enough.

Andy jumped up and placed both hands on the desk. "You mean you're not going to even try any more chemo? What the fuck kind of answer is that?"

Katie touched her husband's taut forearm. "It's an honest answer, darling. It's the kind I want." Andy sat down, his lips pursed in a downward bow.

"We don't think a cure is a realistic hope," Eric said. "It would be best to call hospice."

She nodded, looking at her husband with such transparent love that his lips, which seemed frozen in an expression of barely controlled anger, visibly relaxed.

"Can we have a few minutes to talk about this?" she said.

Both doctors nodded, rose and silently left the room.

Burton and Grueneberg strolled down the hall to the staff lounge.

"You've really gone the extra mile to help Katie," Eric said. "I'd guess all those long-distance conversations and the trips up from Tampa have taken a toll. We've been friends since medical school, and you know I'd do the same for you, but there's more to it than that."

"It's a family debt."

"You mean Katie is related to you?"

Clark's mouth tightened, and he slowly shook his head. "No, it's just that, ever since Dad died, I've thought of him a lot, how he handled tough situations. There's not all that much difference, sometimes, between how generals think and how we doctors deal with crises. We can be pretty cold-blooded for our own protection." He pointed to an enameled lapel pin on his white coat, two crossed flags: Stars and Stripes and a solid red banner with two white stars. "I had a jeweler make this to remind me of Dad."

"I'm not following you."

"Katie's grandfather saved Dad's life." Eric's mouth dropped open, and Clark continued. "Bert Thompson, her grandfather, was Dad's company's first sergeant at Bastogne back in 1944. He took a bullet meant for Dad."

Eric's dark blue eyes stared back through wire-rimmed glasses, like an accountant gazing at a column of figures that didn't quite add up. His eyes brightened. "And your father always remembered that."

"Right. The last time I saw Dad, a few weeks before he died, he reminded me of that debt. I had to tell him that Bert had died just three or four months earlier. He made it clear the obligation was still binding."

Helen Ferguson, the office administrator, came in to get a cup of coffee. Eric took her aside. "Mrs. Lyle's life expectancy is very short. I've recommended that we call hospice. Once I get her approval and her husband's consent, please make the necessary calls. I'll give you a referral letter."

The administrator nodded, turned and walked away. In the silence that descended, her stiletto heels on the hardwood floor sounded like nails being driven into a board...or a coffin.

Helen didn't wait for permission. Immediately upon her return to her office, she picked up her personal cell phone and dialed a number with a few flicks of her thumb.

"Lukas here," a monotone voice answered. "What's new?"

"There's a special referral on the way."

"Particulars?"

She took a deep breath. "It's a young woman. Melanoma, metastasized to the kidneys. Prognosis is terminal, a few weeks maximum."

"Who's the referring physician?"

"She's been under Eric's care for some time. Clark Burton has also been providing care."

"I see. How fast can you get me the paperwork we need? I'll need Dr. G's signature."

"Don't worry, I'll get you a real signature. It'll be here when you need it, an hour at most."

"Any more details I need to know?"

"She has a husband and a four-year-old son."

There was a long silence on the other end of the line. Finally, her interlocutor asked, "Do we need to take special precautions?"

"I think so. No one else needs to be involved except those we can trust."

"Understood. I'll have to bring Diana in on this."

Photo by Barbara V. Evers

"Of course. She knows the importance of discretion." With no further words, she hung up. Leaning back in her chair, she battled the urge to cry.

STEVE GORDY is a college instructor, retired industrial trainer, and aspiring writer. He joined SCWW in 2003 and has been active both at the local chapter level and the state board of directors since then. His current writing project is a novel with the working title *Faith, Hope, and Dr. Vangelis.* Past writing efforts have received recognition from SCWW and writers groups in North Carolina.

The Watchers of Moniah

Barbara V. Evers

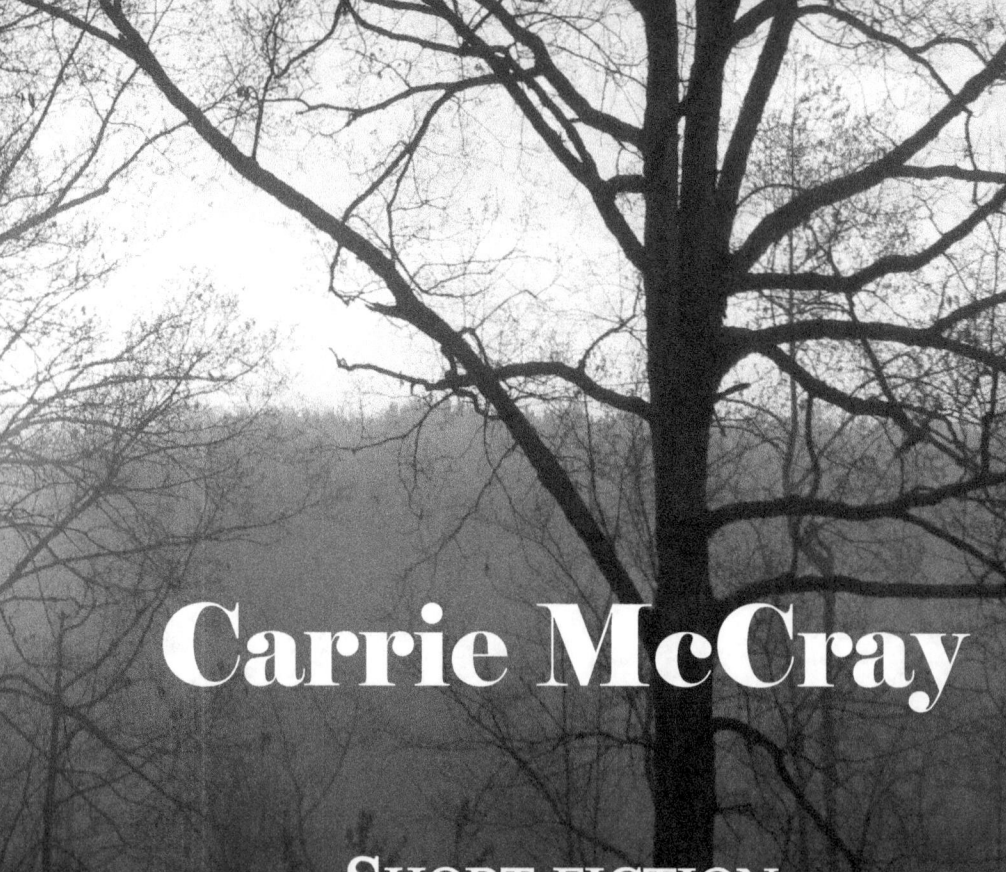

Carrie McCray

SHORT FICTION

Prayers for Bethany

Barbara V. Evers

THE MINUTES TICKED BY IN AGONIZING EONS, drop by drop in time with the saving liquid in the IV bag hung by Bethany's bed in the ICU. Jane, her mother, stared at the fluid wondering how it helped, if it helped, her daughter. The young girl lay on the bed, still and quiet as death, her skin paler than the white sheets hiding most of her injuries.

The steady beep of a machine rang in Jane's ears. A glance at the clock told her only ten minutes had passed since the last time she'd checked, but she couldn't help herself. Never, in a million years, had she expected to sit by the bedside of her only child watching life play a game of hide and seek.

Jane rose and smoothed the hair back from her daughter's forehead, one of the few spots unmarred from the accident. Bob had gone to the crash site and to the junk yard to see the car, the one that boy drove off the road and rolled, her daughter's body bouncing like a rag doll with each screeching impact of metal against ground.

"Mrs. Albright?" A nurse in teddy-bear-covered smocks stood in the doorway. "I need to change her bandages. Why don't you get something from the cafeteria? It will take a while."

Jane heard the unspoken words: You don't want to see these injuries, the damage done to your daughter's arms, legs, her soft belly where Jane gave her zerberts as a baby. Her back, shattered, skin scraped from the surface.

No. Jane wasn't ready to see those things. Not yet. Not ever. She wasn't ready for any of this.

She kissed Bethany's perfect skin in the only safe spot and whispered, "Courage, Bethie, courage. I need you to stay with me."

The smell of blood, of wounds, assaulted Jane's nose in that brief moment. She backed away, breathing deeply, filling her nostrils with the antiseptic and medicinal smells of the hospital. Tears threatened, but she blinked them away with each step backward, her tennis shoes squeaking on the polished floor.

At the door she turned and fled down the hall, barreling through the ICU double doors. She fast-walked past rooms of families dealing with their own crises. She didn't want to know. She didn't want to be there. She wanted to turn back the clock and never see this place.

At the elevator banks the bell chimed the approach of the moving box. When the doors swooshed open, Jane stepped back, making room for a CNA pushing a gurney carrying a toddler. The child laughed at something, startling Jane out of her reverie. The doors dinged shut without admitting her.

She chewed her lip and stared after the child on the gurney. She sagged against the wall, and her purse thumped to the floor. What could she do?

They hadn't known about the boy. Bethany hadn't told them about him. She got in his car, and….

A buzzing sound harassed her, stinging her ankle, until Jane recognized her phone's vibrations. The distance to the phone in her purse stretched below her. She struggled to maintain her balance and yanked open the flap of her bag. She fished around for the insistent rectangle still zapping her leg through the leather sides of her purse. She slid her finger over the screen and placed the cool plastic to her ear. "Hello."

Silence.

"Hello?"

More silence.

A quick glance at the phone showed a missed call message, the number unfamiliar. While she stared at it, the phone buzzed again, announcing a voice mail. Jane swiped the screen and opened the voicemail app. Sixteen messages? She shoved the phone to the bottom of her purse and straightened the strap on her shoulder. With a firm grip on her bag, she jabbed the lit elevator button and jumped when the doors dinged open.

Inside, she turned to choose a floor, but an elderly man beat her to it. "Where to?" he said.

"Um?"

Where was the cafeteria? Did she want to go there?

An expression of sympathy crossed the man's face. "First day?"

She jerked her head down, the best she could do to nod.

"How about the coffee shop?" He bent toward her. "They have sandwiches and much better food than the cafeteria."

"Yes," she said. "Thanks."

Caffeine. The thought created a surge of desire in her veins. She had abstained for months, warned by her doctor, but today wasn't a normal day.

When the elevator doors parted, the man stepped back and gestured her forward. "After you."

Back straight, with quick footsteps, Jane exited the elevator but glanced around in confusion. Where was the coffee shop?

"This way," the man said. "I'm in need of coffee, too." He led her through more double doors and down a hallway that looked familiar. Most of the people in this part of the hospital looked like her. Like they didn't belong. They wore regular clothes. Some stood close, in a huddle. Others stared into space, their hands shoved in their pockets, shoulders hunched to ward off reality. A whiff of cologne streamed from an elderly woman, the stale stink of cigarettes off a rugged-looking couple. Over it all, she still smelled the medicine, Bethany's wounds, and coffee. The rich aroma grew and blanketed her as the man ushered her through a glass door near the main entrance to the hospital.

"Why don't you sit and let me get this for you?" he said, pulling a chair out for her.

Jane obeyed. "Coffee, black."

"A sandwich maybe? They have good egg salad."

She frowned. Hunger was the least of her concerns. "No," she said. As he turned away, she remembered her manners. "Thank you."

A brief sideways nod acknowledged he had heard her.

While he ordered her coffee, Jane studied the man. He stood about Bob's height, just under six feet, a halo of white hair rimming his scalp. The deep wrinkles around his eyes proclaimed him older. The man held his shoulders with the ease of someone comfortable with who he was, aware of his purpose in life. Jane had stood with the same stance just yesterday.

"Here you go." He placed a white mug of coffee in front of her. She wrapped her hands around the ceramic, letting the heat seep into her fingers.

"May I?" He stood beside a chair, his hand hesitating before pulling it out.

"Please." She forced a small smile. "Thank you for helping me."

The man sipped from his cup. A small tassel from a tea bag dangled over the edge. "No problem. We all must help each other when we can." His brown eyes gazed at her as he placed the cup on the table. "You looked like you needed it."

Uncomfortable with his intense gaze, she looked into the deep swirl of coffee, picked up the cup and sipped again.

Her manners nudged her. "Do you have someone here, too?"

It was his turn to look down. A flash of pain crossed his face. It remained in his eyes when he looked back up at her. "I did."

"Oh." Jane's heart gave an agonized beat. She reached for his hand, covering it with her own. His skin, wrinkled with age, felt soft under her carefully manicured hands.

In his pain, this man took care of her. She should have done this for him, not the other way around. "I'm sorry."

"Thank you." He sipped again. "You?"

Ashamed, Jane felt unable to deny him the information. "My daughter. She's sixteen."

"So young," he said. His confident shoulders sagged under the weight of his world and hers added to it.

"Yes."

They sat for a moment, each tracing patterns over the handles of their cups, neither drinking. Jane glanced at her watch. Somehow, the minutes had passed. The nurse should be done with the bandages by the time she returned to ICU.

He caught her glance. "Time to go back?"

Jane shrugged. It was nice to sit quietly with someone. Bob had tried, but his anger at the boy boiled around the room and made Jane anxious. Finally, she had told Bob to go home, get some rest, do some work. His face looked relieved as he left.

But this man, in the midst of his own pain, a man she didn't even know, gave her the peace she needed.

"They have a chapel on this floor," he said. "I was headed there when I saw you. Would you like to join me?"

Jane smiled at his understanding. "Yes. Please." She reached for her purse. "How much do I owe you?"

"Nothing." He waved her offer away. "If you're a praying woman, maybe you'll pray for my son?"

"You lost him?" Her heart ached with the knowledge of how this must hurt, how close she stood to losing her own child.

"Oh no. No." The man sighed. "He lost his son. My grandson."

Words didn't come to her. She brushed his hand again in sympathy.

They ambled along to the chapel, neither speaking.

The doors swung open to a dimly lit room. An aisle ran down the middle of five rows of pews. Candles burned on an altar, a huge Bible opened between them. Jane slid into a hard pew and folded her hands in her lap. "What is your son's name?"

The man didn't answer. He had approached the altar and stood before the Bible, his arms held toward the heavens. He prayed in a soft, but firm voice that echoed in the chamber. "Father, my heart aches, it cracks under the pressure. Please, comfort my son, Jonah. Help him through this loss. And, please embrace our Keith in your arms. Welcome him home to heaven. I pray that my Linda is there to show him your kingdom and to ease his fears."

There was a pause as the man's shoulders heaved. His voice cracked, and for a moment he gave a wordless cry that drove deep into the core of Jane's soul. She bit her lip, and tears welled in her eyes.

Ashamed at eavesdropping, Jane bowed her head to pray.

The man spoke again, his voice an urgent whisper. "And God, please, please heal the little girl in Keith's car. Please, God, I pray for Bethany."

Photo from Pixabay - CCO Public Domain

BARBARA V. EVERS loves books. When she's not reading or writing, she works as a professional trainer and public speaker. She holds an MA in Professional Communication and is a Certified MBTI Instructor. Barbara's short stories and essays appear in *Child of My Child*, *The Petigru Review*, the *moonShine review*, and *Stupefying Stories*. She contributes regularly to five blogs, two of which are her own personal sites. She is an active member of South Carolina Writers' Workshop where she served three years on the board and now leads a local chapter.

Rehab

Douglas Wyant

"WHAT HAPPENED TO YOU, SON?"

I opened my eyes. A scrawny man slouched in a wheelchair parked against the opposite wall. I studied his wizened features, a smoker's face, partially covered with a scant, grizzled beard.

"I'm not your son," I said.

"You're mighty tetchy this morning," he said. At least that's what I heard.

He prodded me with another question.

Before I could unscramble his words, a lady clad in gray sweatpants and pink sweatshirt answered for me. "He was in that wreck on the Fourth."

The old man's shriveled face lit up. "We saw the report on the evening news. A highway patrolman clocked you at ninety. He said the truck rolled three times. You're lucky to be alive."

I didn't consider myself lucky. He knew more about the accident than I remembered.

After lunch, while we waited for our next therapy sessions, a robust man dressed in a charcoal-gray suit, wearing an emblem that identified him as a minister, breezed through the room, dispensing cheerful benedictions.

My family was never very religious. An acquaintance once asked why we didn't attend weekly worship services. Daddy said, "I don't like to be preached at."

Although he was not a believer, Daddy faithfully observed the first day of the week as a day of rest. Sundays, we slept late.

The Sunday Daddy fixed breakfast – fried ham and eggs, grits and red-eye gravy, biscuits slathered with butter, orange juice and coffee, even though mine was mostly milk – lingers in my memory. Mother entered the kitchen singing "Happy Birthday," and I blew out all ten candles on the chocolate cake with one breath.

That morning, while Mother washed and rinsed the dishes, and I dried and put them away, Daddy walked downtown to purchase a copy of the *State* paper.

Daddy had not returned home by nightfall, when I came in for supper, after playing outside all afternoon.

Mother called all our friends. She called the hospital. She called the police. She even called the pastor of the church we had only attended for weddings and funerals.

No one had seen him. He just vanished, as if he had been abducted by aliens.

Day by day, years passed.

As if afraid Daddy wouldn't be able to find us, Mother refused to move. Until she retired on disability at fifty-nine, she waited tables at local restaurants.

After I graduated from high school, I went away to college on a football scholarship. Although we had a so-so season my freshman year, Mother never came to any of our games.

My athletic career and my college education ended my sophomore year. I married a girl I met on a blind date and we moved to her hometown. When our marriage fizzled out, she drifted to Florida, but I stayed on in Pousto, which is as good a place as any I've ever been, and better than most. After 9/11, I trained to be a first responder.

On the July Fourth, the temperature hovered near one hundred, as it had all week. At the community picnic, I'd just loaded a paper plate with baked beans, potato salad, coleslaw—and a grilled cheeseburger, when my pager started beeping.

Ten minutes later I parked my pickup in the driveway of a white frame house less than five miles from my apartment. As soon as I opened the truck door, the stench engulfed me.

The screen door banged against the side of the house and a man scuttled across the front porch and heaved the contents of his stomach over the banister into the shrubs. When he stood up, I recognized Captain Magee, who has a reputation for his cast-iron constitution.

All the windows were black, covered inside with millions of flies. I found their host in bed, lying on his back, an open Bible face down on his chest and an empty whiskey bottle beside him. A small tarnished frame on the bedside table held a black-and-white, wallet-size photograph of my mother and me.

DOUGLAS WYANT has received a Scott Lax Wildacres Scholarship and a Carrie McCray Memorial Literary Award from SCWW. His fiction has been published in *The Petigru Review* and *moonShine review*. One of his stories was nominated for a Pushcart Prize. He was a finalist for the 2014 American Fiction Short Story Award.

Carrie McCray

CREATIVE NONFICTION

Listening to Her Breathe

Valerie Keiser Norris

WE GET THE PHONE CALL ON A SUNDAY. My husband's mother, Ella, has had a stroke.

She ignored colon cancer until it encased her liver, and her options are bleak. Chemo will give her a little more time, but she'll never improve enough to leave the hospital. Or, she can go home with hospice care and perhaps have a week.

She wants to go home.

Her husband is weak and feeble, in the midst of chemo for lung cancer. John's divorced brother is on crutches from a knee replacement. Hospice will handle nursing and relief care, but we must come. We arrange time off work, throw clothes in suitcases and head north from Georgia to Michigan. When we're too tired to drive we stop at a motel for a little sleep and drive on the next day.

On Monday morning we arrive at the hospital. Ella holds our hands and talks to us, her voice a croak issuing from a misshapen mouth. Her upper lip puffs out, more of a beak than a lip. Swelling from the stroke?

When did she get so thin, so frail? Her right wrist is tiny, blue-veined. Her left hand, the stroke side, is swollen.

A therapist comes in to work on her recovery. A nurse tells us of the importance of turning her often and keeping sheets wrinkle-free to avoid bedsores.

Recovery? Bedsores? Did we misunderstand the prognosis? How long does she have? As Ella's gurney is wheeled from the hospital room to the transport van, everyone stares at us. I wonder if they know we're taking her home to die.

The transport people bring the gurney up the four steps into her house and lay her in the hospital bed in the middle of the living room. The door closes behind them, and I'm frightened by the responsibility of her care. She's swaddled like a baby, but when I try to unwrap her she groans in pain. I decide to wait for the hospice people to help.

The hospice nurse and another woman come, unwrap all the sheets, and find that Ella has soiled herself. They explain how to roll her to her side and clean her with wipes. At their directions I scurry to locate wash-cloths, a man's T-shirt, scissors, Vaseline for her lips, a glass of water. Lukewarm, I'm told. Not cold.

They cut the back of the T-shirt from hem to collar so they can cover her without pulling anything over her head. From the waist down only bedding shields her, and a big blue pad lies beneath her. A catheterization line leads to a bag already collecting urine.

John stands in the archway to the dining room, eyes averted.

The nurse tells Ella, "We're going to the kitchen to sign papers."

Ella is determined to join them. She has already asked to be taken to the kitchen where she and John's step-father have spent so much time over the years, sitting at the table smoking cigarettes.

"John can help me," she insists.

I explain that she and I are not going to the kitchen.

"John can take me," she insists again.

"Your left side is paralyzed," I remind her. "You'll fall out of the chair."

"John can hold me."

I tell her I'm sorry.

Our youngest daughter, Ali, and her husband arrive from North Carolina. Ella holds and kisses hands as if desperate to express the love she's held inside for as long as I've known her.

After the hospice folks leave I must clean Ella. She pushes my hands away and shakes her head. "You shouldn't do this."

"It's John, Jim, your husband, or me," I say. "I think you want me. Besides, this is what women do. We take care of others." I need John to help roll her to her side. His mother isn't heavy, but she's dead weight. Again, he carefully averts his gaze. As her face gets close to the side of the bed she panics.

"Don't drop me. Don't break my hip."

I'm afraid of that, too.

To pass the time I read to her from a murder mystery open on the end table. When I mention blood, she winces. It's too gory.

So I search her shelves – all murder mysteries. I borrow *The Hobbit* from my daughter and read a few paragraphs before Ella dozes off.

When she wakes, she worries whether the beds have clean sheets, about where we will sleep. When I walk by with a load of laundry she asks, "What are you washing?"

Later, I fold and put away bras, sweatshirts and pants she'll never wear again.

Somehow the fingernails on her right hand have gotten filthy, crescents of black under each nail. I find a nail brush and fill a basin of soapy water, clean both of her hands and follow up with lotion. She calls me her angel, kisses my hand and falls asleep. Her mouth never closes completely, and each breath is audible.

John is lying on the short love seat, his knees raised high to fit his six-foot plus length. I tell him to go upstairs and nap.

"I'm listening to her breathe," he says. "It's kind of comforting."

In the evening Ella says, "Do you sing?"

I sing, "Toora Loora Looral," an Irish lullaby my mother sang.

The phone rings, and I ask Ali to take over. I leave the room to talk to our eldest daughter. When I return, Ali's husband, Ella's husband and John have migrated to the living room to listen to Ali's clear soprano.

"Wonderful, beautiful," Ella says over and over and kisses her granddaughter's hand. "My baby."

I nap from 9:00 PM until 11:30 PM, then take over for John. Through the night I doze for an hour in the recliner, then wake up to check on her, talk to her, offer water on a sponge-wand, more meds. She denies pain, but still groans as I attempt to clean her. At 4:30 AM she seems out of it, and I can no longer understand her. Worried, I call hospice, and they ask if I've read the booklet. What booklet? I find it in the kitchen and learn what to expect.

In the morning Ali and her husband say their goodbyes and head home. A neighbor stands on the sidewalk in front of the house, and I go out to explain the situation. She doesn't ask to come in. None of the neighbors, folks Ella and her husband have known for thirty years, approach the house.

A hospice pastor comes to pray with Ella, and a nurse drops by. Cece, our hospice worker, comes at 1:00 PM, bathes Ella and dresses her in a clean shirt sliced up the back. I ask about bedsores.

"Hospitals have rules about that. We aim for comfort." She calls the office about Ella's cough and congestion, concerned about pneumonia. Again I wonder about the timeline. Isn't she dying?

Amber, our middle daughter, who is getting married in two weeks, calls, in tears about her grandmother and about the wedding. I assure her that, no matter what, we will be there for her wedding.

The Hobbit is gone with Ali, so I find another book and read aloud. When Ella falls asleep, I stop, but her husband, resting in the recliner, says, "I was listening." I keep reading.

Wednesday morning she's very hard to understand. She keeps pointing and saying, "You *(mumble mumble)*." She tries three or four times. Helpless, I strain to understand.

A few friends come by, but it's an awkward visit.

Ella's right eye begins to wink. It happens enough that I ask if she's winking at me. Then both eyes get in on the act, big, exaggerated blinks. She sleeps. One eye will not close. I decide the blinks signaled another stroke.

That evening John takes me out to dinner, leaving Ella in the care of her husband and Jim. I cry three times on the way to the restaurant, feeling I've abandoned her.

After dinner, I sleep a few hours, until 1:10 AM. When I enter the living room, Ella's breathing is louder, labored. Not comforting. John wants to stay up, certain she will pass soon. After a few minutes, he admits exhaustion and goes to bed.

I give her the liquid pain medicine and speak in a soothing tone. "John's gone to bed, Valerie's here, I'll be with you all night. You won't be alone...."

She begins deep, gasping breaths, slower, slower. This might be it. I want to get John, but if I leave will she die alone? Did she choose this time, when her sons and husband are out of the room? When she had mumbled "You something something," is that what she tried to tell me? Did she want to save them from this moment?

I hold her hand, sing "Amazing Grace," tell her she worked hard all her life and now is going to her reward. That we will all be fine, she doesn't need to worry.

And then she is gone.

I wake John and his step-father, call Jim and hospice. Cece comes to talk with us. She suggests we leave the room while the funeral home people "do the next part." When the house is quiet, we come back to an empty room. A rose is on the hospital bed's pillow.

Ella's husband makes a pot of coffee, the Michigan response to every situation. We sit at the kitchen table and drink coffee until he is ready to go back to sleep.

At 5:00 AM I fall into bed, but sleep is far from me. I think back over the last few days and realize that this crisis is the first time I've felt as if Ella and I were mother and daughter.

And I'm not sure which was which.

VALERIE KEISER NORRIS moved south 28 years ago with her husband and three daughters. She won the 2013 Hub City/EMRYS Creative Writing prize, the 2009 Carrie McCray fiction contest and Honorable Mention twice in *Writer's Digest* Fiction Competitions. Several stories have appeared in anthologies (*Sweeter Than Tea* and *A Stone Mountain Christmas*). A novel excerpt, "Satan's Lingerie," won an award and was published in *The Petigru Review*, but somehow hasn't resulted in a book publishing contract. She's had short stories, articles and humor published in small magazines and occasionally posts to a humorous blog at ValerieNorris.blogspot.com.

On the Clock

Bob Strother

THE WALL CLOCK LOOMS just over the doorway as if it were a sentinel charged with monitoring ingress and egress, rendering judgment on those who pass underneath: *Your* time here will be quick and bubbly – effervescent with nervous laughter until the doors open and you shriek with excitement and smile at the little bundle of wonderment you've helped create; or, *your* tenure here will be interminable, as if by slowing the drift of time, you will have even longer to suffer the uncertainty of what the future holds.

What will *I* hold when this night is over?

Will it be like the last time, when all I held was hope? Which ultimately turned out to be the cruelest torture of all.

I watch the clock, admire its simplicity: round and ringed with silver, like the moon, and enveloped by the wispy clouds from my cigarette—the first cigarette I've smoked in months because the smell sickened my pregnant wife. After this night—if it ever ends, *however* it ends—I *will* smoke again, and probably my wife will as well.

The clock hands are black and seem permanently fixed on three-forty-two. I've been here since seven-twenty-four. The pains started just after dinner. Dinner seems like yesterday. Actually it was yesterday, and I suppose whatever happens tonight should feel like tomorrow.

But tomorrow never comes, does it?

BOB STROTHER is a two-time Pushcart Prize nominee and his work has
been published widely and internationally. His short story "Doughnut
Walk"— originally published in the 2011 Petigru *Review* — was recently
adapted for film. Previous publications include a short story collection,
Scattered, Smothered, and Covered and a novel-in-stories, *Shug's Place*. His new
novel, *Burning Time*, is scheduled for release later this year. Strother is also
a contributing writer for *Southern Writers Magazine*. He lives with his wife,
Vicki, in Greenville, South Carolina.

Carrie McCray

Contest Judges

FIRST CHAPTER OF A NOVEL

Courtney McKinney-Whitaker

COURTNEY MCKINNEY-WHITAKER is from Greenville, SC. She spent most of her early adulthood trying to avoid writing books by going to grad school and working as a librarian, composition teacher and writing consultant. Her debut novel, *The Last Sister*, published by Young Palmetto Books at the University of South Carolina Press, tied for the 2015 IPPY silver medal in historical fiction. Follow her online.

CourtneyMckinneyWhitaker.com
Facebook: courtneymckinneywhitakerauthor
Twitter: @courtneymckwhit

"I feel so honored to be trusted with judging this year's First Chapter contest and want to thank all the authors for the opportunity to read your work. No matter how much you've been published, it takes great courage to send your writing into the world, and the greatest reward is the company of a community of writers all seeking to improve our craft. Congratulations.

SHORT FICTION

Jessica Probus

JESSICA PROBUS is a writer, editor and designer living in New York City. Her work can be found on *BuzzFeed, McSweeneys, Word Riot, The Rumpus, Nano Fiction, The Billfold* and *Homepolish.*

NONFICTION

Nathan Jandl

NATHAN JANDL is a scholar, writer, editor, and photographer who lives in Madison, WI with his wife, the novelist Chloe Benjamin. He is completing his PhD in English at the University of Wisconsin-Madison, where he also serves as Managing Editor for *Edge Effects*, the official blog for the Center for Culture, History, and Environment. Nathan's writing has appeared in *The Believer*, *Ninth Letter*, *Midwestern Gothic*, and elsewhere, and he was a finalist for the *Crazyhorse* Nonfiction Prize in 2014. For more information and to view his photography, visit NathanJandl.com.

"It was a pleasure and an honor to review this year's submissions for the Carrie McCray Memorial Literary Award in nonfiction. The quality and breadth of nonfiction being written today is simply remarkable, and this contest was a prime example of that. Congratulations to all!

TPR

Poetry

Photo by Edith Hawkins

Business Dreams Involving Inordinately Small Song Birds

Elaine Holliday

I wanted to be the middle man
of buying and selling tiny, tiny, *tiny* canaries.
These canaries – quite pretty, quite yellow,
singing songs your dogs could shake a tail at,
could be led through your nose
and be your first-alert for a cold or sinus infection.
That is what I would tell the retailers. Buy, buy birdy.
And to my suppliers
I would front and scoff and spit and laugh,
Those? Those are not tiny, tiny canaries.
What are those, gills? What are those, elephants?
I can only purchase the cutest, the sweetest,
the most asthmatic.
But then the government came in
and wrote those damn bills.
What am I going to do
with all these tiny, tiny, *tiny* bird cages?

Watch Credits

Elaine Holiday

I am an owl-faced box,
keep my eyes in my pockets –
used to fear dust.
Now all I see
is the clatter of dimes.
All day long,
I'm turning my head around.
Used to be small like carpet fibers.
Used to hear the skittering of every
creature, every creature's nail clinging
to this world, every fierce wind
snapping them up or
snapping at them.
Used to laugh at them.
Used to know their time, my time
was *the* time
and I counted all of it:
every 10 minutes was
another dime in the payphone
and I had a mind
like a rotary phone –
always going back to home.
Used to be fresh
like a September fig.

Used to be the jewel
in my breast plate.
Used to carry myself
proudly out on nice summer days.
Used to have all sorts of strangers come up to me
and coo.

Photo from Pixabay - CCO Public Domain

Photo by Irena Tervo

Grandma Speaks Up

Kathryn Etters Lovatt

What do I know of this land,
no different than any other
except it's yours, before you,
your father's, and before that,
sumac and grapes, snakes
hiding under logs or coming
up the steps to snatch a kitten.

I finish one meal, begin the next,
boil jars and gather my lids.
I drag out the broom.
I'm your servant and the earth's.

The sand records drought or rain,
the tire trails and wild prints
of whatever comes and goes,
but you, who's yet to put a toilet roll
around an empty spool, carry this ground
in your cock's crow
and on the bottom of your boots.

You track dirt everywhere,
and leave me to gather its grains
on this side of the door,
throw it back to the other.

Deep Sea

Len Lawson

Deep calleth unto deep at the noise of Thy waterspouts: all Thy waves and Thy billows are gone over me.

Psalm 42:7, King James Version

Eyes still breathe under water
Just through prisms like marbles
They see the world as ocean

Galaxies of vision
Beckoning sky and sea
Heaven and deep

Ascending and descending
I thought my eyes drowned
Staring at Daddy's body

On that ER bed
My sister's eyes too
Mama never reached out to save our eyes

She also never said if Daddy's eyes
Reached out for us before returning to the deep
I haven't blinked to find out

Photo from Pixabay - CCO Public Domain

Photo by Jayne Bowers

Uncle J's Blues

Len Lawson

He had two daughters
seven years apart
no son yet

lost his finger and bike in a
motorcycle accident
still had his white Mustang Cobra

took off his cool before Daddy's wake
long enough to wear me as
his black leather vest

walking up Hunters Chapel Road
peering down at me through
aviator sunglasses

It wasn't about how many beers
he and Daddy knocked back or
how many they'd never knock back again

I was the boy he never had that day
I thought I became his phantom finger too
No, I became the nub that would

never grow back

Dream in Color

Leah Brown

I dream in color
        (though black and white is beautiful)

The periwinkle blue of the sky
        on a humid, hazy day
And granny-smith-apple green
        so tart I can taste it
Burgundy, moss green, or emerald
        ruby, topaz, and sapphire

The sapphire blue of the water
that I endlessly swam for six years

Night
        after night
                after night

Broad lakes and piers
connected to houses and stores
The only mode of travel?
Swimming

Night
        after night
                after night

Six long years of keeping my head above water

Barely
        exhaustingly
                persistently

But the blue
        the beautiful sapphire blue

I dream in color
        (though black and white is beautiful)

Photo by Jayne Bowers

Miami Cold

Carol-Ann Rudy

When it's cold in Miami
lizards stick to the window
like licorice to my teeth
and air takes on the crackle
of champagne drunk from crystal,
no longer languid on my tongue.
Color flattens, cheap prints of a Master's,
and the moon over Rickenbacker
jumps up yellow.

When it's cold in Miami
bathing beauties sport goosebumps
like strange fruit blossoming
and sugared praline sand crunches between my toes
inviting them to linger.
Hot café Cubano tongues me
leaving me senseless,
and the moon over Rickenbacker
jumps up yellow.

When it's cold in Miami
wind flies from flagpoles
jousting with pelicans,
joking with the waves and stitching ruffles at water's edge.
Needles of cold air kiss my legs that dance between yours on Calle Ocho
and I am swallowed up in love with the night, the stars, and you,
when the moon over Rickenbacker
jumps up yellow.

Photo by Averette - Licensed under CC

Poem in Lent for Jack

Michael Hugh Lythgoe

(for Kathy)

A friend slipped away to become a ghost
among other poor souls. We gather
at a round table to break bread.
We go quiet to remember Jack.
When he began to feel a slow trouble
in his brain, he could not focus on a crocus
or a cottage: *I just want to listen to Opera.*
His wife was with him. His children
came from out of town, for the end.
Sometimes there is a bomb in our ceiling.
We never know when it will go off,
or if. It is hard to breathe again –
pollen in the air like gold dust. Birds
sing everywhere, trill to nest in a wreath
on the front door. New leaves
are not yet there. Wisteria drips purple
shades like draped statues before Palm Sunday.
Rains and wind scatter cherry pink tatters.
The church reminds us of Noah's dove –
the image of the Holy Ghost
on this Friday in the 5th week of Lent.
He just wants to hear opera.
Three strange angels come with redbuds.
Let them in to tell of choirs, resurrection.

Sonnet for New Year

Michael Hugh Lythgoe

January opens stainless steel sky.
Janus barges in after artillery,
looks both ways, delivers a cold cargo.
I drive for coffee, hear guitar, gypsy
music airs; a posse gathers – Harley
bikers – compare steeds, and stables, parley.
Equestrians shoot the breeze; a jockey,
a woman trainer takes coffees to go.
Pisces – my sign – heads or tails, sink or flow.
On The *Writer's Almanac* – a litany,
remedy for Hemingway-hangover.
Audubon time for bird watchers, counters.
Life wears two masks: comedy, tragedy.
Face back, see ahead; faith is no malady.

Salvage Man

Michael Hugh Lythgoe

(for C. Y.)

He roars up in his pickup.
I'm shooting pictures of his junk
yard cars near the highway. Posted.
No permission slip. What is in
the pics belongs to him he says.
I apologize. He settles down.

Mr. C. has stories to share –
he drove a wrecker, like his father,
his grandson calls it an escalator;
he owns the land both sides of Whiskey Road –
named for bootleggers who
drove 10 gallon barrels on once
unpaved roads. Robbers now steal
& tow off prized salvage from pine
straw. I admire derelict Dodges, Ford
Fairlane, big old chrome bumpers –
bright silver flashes in sunlight.
He talks a long time about life
as a trucker, laborer in a textile mill,
hauling fuel to the nuclear bomb site,
being "badged," being a breaker
of wrecked cars. He cut them
in three pieces & hauled away wrecks
3 at a time on his truck. I like
all the remnants of Chryslers.

My father worked at a Chrysler plant.
My first car was a Dodge Dart.

We trade names, depart as friends.
I leave Atomic Auto Parts, drive
rusty stories away, photos of a '74 Dodge,
damaged, SC centennial plates. Memory
of another wreck: Black ice, 1969 Ford Galaxy,
sleek tail fins. 3 strange angels rescued my wife.
Collectors eyed prize towed to salvage.

Photo by Michael Hugh Lythgoe

Self Rising

Donna Wylie

Captured in a web
of maternal love,
shaped within the mold
of her expectations,

I clung to Mama
for a full measure of worth,
a cookie left
too long to bake.

Stumbled over
buried feelings,
inside a burned
out love.

Papa sprinkled crumbs
of affection into
my starved heart.

The hunger for fatherly approval
led me on an endless path
of nameless, faceless men.

They consumed me
when I exchanged
who I am
for raw attention.

I prayed for
a soul mate
to feed me.

My own
sustenance
answered the call.

Photo by Jayne Bowers

Thread

Jennifer Bartell

Tears sprinkle her not yet cold
skin. The hospice house is quiet.
Tropical Storm Ernesto dumps
rain on us. My father cries
Don't leave me, Bobbie!

Bobbie, don't leave me!
          but she has already left.

We wait for the funeral home.
I lie down in the hospital bed
next to her not yet cold body
and rub the back of her hands.
Her jaundiced eyes do not close,

even when I put my hand
over them like they do
in the movies.
Still.
I try to close her eyes
because I don't want her to
see what comes next.

She may be dead, but she's not
blind. On this bed,
she smells like her living self.

The funeral home is here.
I watch them zip
her up in the black bag.

She kept a brown and black
purse as a sewing kit. While
looking for a needle,
I open it,
bury my head in it.
This is it.

How she smelled.
Her purse always
had her scent.

I hope to hem in this smell,
                    but it has already left.

Photo by Edith Hawkins

FICTION

Photo by Jayne Bowers

Holy Vows

Valerie Keiser Norris

THE CLEAN SCENT of yeast rises up from the dough she has stopped kneading. Against the backdrop of soft acoustic guitar the raspy, deep voice sings to her. She has never liked these songs: *Puff the Magic Dragon,* and one about a cake left out in the rain. But he sings softly, and her hands falter on the dough. She imagines herself next to him on the wicker settee at the far end of her kitchen, her head thrown back and eyes closed, as his are.

He showed up half an hour earlier from his house next door. "Are you busy? I haven't sung in front of an audience in a long time."

Their families are frequently in each other's homes for casual dinners, pizza nights and outdoor fire pit gatherings. But this is different. The house is empty except for the two of them. Kids in school, husband at work.

The cat's away, the mice will play?

He looks up. "Are you done?"

She shakes her head no.

"Good. I need more practice."

She takes an unsteady breath. Gather the dough, press with the heels of the hands. Gather, press. Gather, press. Breathe.

He sings "The Wedding Song," about a man leaving his father and a woman leaving her home....

Her heart races, a deer fleeing a gunshot, a wild mustang escaping capture. Could she have a heart attack from someone singing a love song? She stares down at her hands, lying still once again. Grooves are deeply embedded into the ring finger of her left hand, the evidence of a binding relationship even when the rings sit in the dish on the kitchen windowsill.

He packs his guitar in its case and leaves with an awkward goodbye. She runs to the bathroom, weeping. Small explosions wrack her chest, her stomach, her throat, and she presses her hands against her mouth. Staring in the mirror at her frantic eyes, she has an urge to laugh in the midst of her tears. Look at you! Forty-five years old, overweight, married. Mooning over your friend's husband.

Shamed, she washes away the evidence of tears.

For two days and nights it is all she can think about. You're a ridiculous old fool, she tells herself as she rubs lotion on crow's feet and brushes her gray-shot hair. At night she lies rigid next to the man who held her hand during childbirth, while they waited for biopsy results and during her father's funeral. The man she might betray.

In the dark she is vibrant and attractive. She fantasizes about kissing a new mouth, touching a new body.

Next to her, her husband begins his soft snore.

Her period starts, and the frenzy fades. Her husband is a quiet, gentle, good man. They have a family, a history, a life. When he makes quiet, gentle love to her, she is able to put the whole incident in perspective. It is harmless, a passing attraction aggravated by hormone crazies.

It happens again six weeks later.

He comes by without his guitar. "I wanted to thank you for letting me practice here," he says. "I didn't win, but the talent show went well." He meets her gaze. She cannot look away.

In the space of a moment, twenty-five years of marriage, fidelity, trust, drop away like dried rose petals. Future plans, family Christmases with as-yet-unborn grandchildren, growing old together: all of it falls to the floor in a crumbling, dusty heap. She stares at his face, which mirrors her own hope and terror. This can't happen. But a voice asks how long it has been since a man looked at her with such open longing, such *want*?

The front door slams. "Mom, I'm home."

She turns away from him and forces a happy greeting for her daughter. When the friend leaves she flees to the bathroom, the only witness to her overreactions. She covers her mouth with her hand, silent in her grief, in her joy.

In a little while her breathing evens, her body stops shaking. She knows she must return to the kitchen and ask about her daughter's day. Her absence is more telling than words. But for another moment she leans her head back against the wall, eyes closed, mouth slightly open as if for a deep kiss.

He wants her. It is heaven. It is misery. It is enough.

Photo from Flickr.com © 2009 by Ben Grey CC License

Photo by Irena Tervo

The Summer I Heard the Drumming

Bob Strother

I PREFER TO CALL IT the winter of my discontent, primarily because *The Winter of Our Discontent* was the last novel I happened to finish before flunking out of college in the winter of 1970. Despite the many parallels I found between myself and Steinbeck's protagonist, Ethan Hawley, my stepfather had a less philosophical take on the situation: "A goddamn waste of money," he called it.

So I left the University of Georgia mid-January and slunk home to Macon and a house divided. My mother wanted me to attend classes at the University Extension in Marietta and retake the courses I'd failed – the only way I could return to the Athens campus in the fall. My stepfather wanted me to work for a while and learn to "appreciate the value of a hard-earned dollar."

I didn't mind working, but didn't relish the idea of losing my draft deferment. No matter what Nixon promised to get elected, there were still no signs the war was slowing down in Viet Nam. In the end, my mom lost the argument.

"I can get you on at the factory," my stepfather said. "But you'll have to pull your own weight. It'll look bad for me if you don't." He worked as a maintenance electrician at Crane Company, a leading manufacturer of sinks, bathtubs, and other bathroom products. It was shift work – hard, hot and dirty.

The matter seemed closed until a couple of days later when my mom announced over dinner that her brother in Akron had offered me a temporary job at his print shop. "It's more than minimum wage, Greg," she said to my stepfather, "which is all he'd make at Crane. And with overtime, he'll probably make enough to pay for summer classes at the Extension."

I glanced at Greg, expecting to hear a protest. Instead, I saw a look of relief come over his face. Maybe it was because he wouldn't need to worry about me "measuring up on the job." It might've also been the money I'd make, which wouldn't have to come out of his pocket. Or maybe he'd just gotten used to a house without a teenager around. Whatever it was, it didn't matter. I was relieved, too.

It was colder in Akron than Macon, but the weeks went by, and the weather warmed considerably by late April. My uncle's print shop business was booming, and I had all the overtime I wanted. I spoke to my mother at least once a week, always hoping I hadn't received a draft notice in the mail. Between helping with the presses and making deliveries, I didn't have much time for listening to the news, but the radio was playing late in the afternoon on April 30 when President Nixon announced the invasion of Cambodia by US troops.

"That son of a bitch Nixon," my uncle said, taping a box of printed materials. He glanced at me. "Excuse my French, Tommy, but that lying bastard is going out of his way to get more of our boys killed."

"It's all right, Uncle Boyd. I've heard worse."

He went back about his tasks, mumbling under his breath.

I'm not sure I knew what to think about the war in Viet Nam. In truth, I hadn't given it much thought while I was in school. Now, with the specter of the draft hanging over my head, it seemed much closer to home.

A few days later, my uncle gestured to several stacks of cardboard boxes next to the loading platform out back. "I need you to run these up to the university in Kent. You'll see signs directing you to Prentice Hall. It's room 214."

It was close to 11:30 when I arrived at the campus and found my way through the Prentice Hall parking lot to a section marked for deliveries. Across a wide expanse I assumed must be the Commons, a large group of students had congregated, and more were flocking to the area. Beyond the mass, a smaller group of men in olive drab uniforms were visible, and beyond them, a convergence of campus police and military vehicles.

Inside Prentice Hall, while pushing a hand truck loaded with boxes, I came upon a middle-aged woman staring out the through the building's double glass doors.

"What's going on out there?" I said.

"It's a protest rally against the war," she said, a frown creasing her forehead. "We had a small one a few days ago, but this one's much larger. The National Guard is here."

I made three trips unloading boxes, then headed back to the truck. Meanwhile, the conglomeration of students flowed back and forth, moving amoeba-like between the Commons, the Prentice Hall parking lot and an adjacent classroom building. Police and guardsmen followed, shouting into loudspeakers for the students to disperse. The students yelled back – "Pigs off campus" – and tossed rocks at the soldiers.

A pretty girl hurried past me toward the growing mob – her long auburn hair adorned with a wreath of woven white pansies. "Come on," she yelled to me over her shoulder. "Let's stop this fucking war."

I was torn between watching the spectacle of the protest – something I couldn't imagine ever happening at the University of Georgia – and some innate sense of self-preservation. When a smoking tear gas canister rolled to within a few yards of me, self-preservation won out. I scrambled into the delivery truck and edged my way slowly toward the exit. It wasn't easy – clamoring protestors darted back and forth in front of me. Several times I thought I'd be trapped in the chaos, but eventually I spied the turnout and floored the gas pedal. A guardsman stood nearby, his rifle at the ready. I slowed again to make the turn, but he waved me on, shouting, "Go, go, go."

When I was on the road leading to the main campus entrance, the confrontation was still visible through my open side window. Shouts of protest from the students alternated with the squawk of bullhorns. The guardsmen had regrouped near the Commons when a phalanx of protestors advanced on them from behind the classroom building adjacent to Prentice Hall.

A single shot rang out, followed by what sounded like a string of firecrackers exploding. A few seconds later the screaming started.

Uncle Boyd and his wife and I watched it all on CBS that evening: four students killed, nine injured. Reports of what happened varied greatly, accompanied by breaking speculation from a coterie of experts and journalists. Shrouded in a frenzy of finger-pointing, the incident was termed a "tragic occurrence" by all concerned.

Toward the end of May, I returned to Macon with enough money to enroll for makeup classes at the UGA Extension in Marietta. It was exactly what my mother had hoped for, but I didn't have the stomach for it. Instead, I took a summer job at Crane Company, loading, unloading, and stacking bathtubs.

The third shift foreman had a sign he kept tacked to his work station: "College boys – put mind in motion before putting mouth in gear." I was bruised, scraped, and exhausted, and the work was mind-numbing, but I didn't care. On our dinner break, although I was no longer one of them, I hung out with the summer college-guy workers. We drank ice-cold Sprites, smoked cigarettes and listened to Neil Young's protest song, released shortly after the Kent State massacre. He sang about hearing drumming and four dead.

Over the next two months, one of my colleagues lost a knuckle stacking tubs, one was sent to the hospital after getting "white-eyed" from the heat and passing out, and another simply quit without notice. Greg came around sometimes. He didn't say much, just talked with the foreman and nodded occasionally in my direction. When one of the older men rolled to the second shift, I took his job stenciling the Crane Company logo on porcelain-glazed bathtubs still steaming from the baking ovens. It was an extra fifteen cents an hour, and while my stepfather never told me so directly, I believe he was proud.

My draft notice arrived on August 16, and I left for basic training shortly afterward. My mom cried, of course, and even Greg's lower lip trembled a bit when he shook my hand and gave my shoulder a rare pat.

On the bus to Fort Benning I thought a lot about what had happened in Ohio and what might happen yet in Viet Nam, my most probable first deployment. None of it made much sense to me, and probably never would. I wasn't all that smart, and there were plenty of analysts and intellectuals who might spend months or even years trying to sort it all out. I also pondered what it would be like to spend my working life sweating through a swing shift job at Crane Company or some other similar industry. Maybe, by the time I came home, it would be safe to go back onto a college campus.

For the next couple of years, though, I'd have much more pressing priorities – like staying alive.

Flight

M.Z. Thwaite

A TOUSLED BLONDE HEAD ADJUSTED on the pillow. Unnatural silence lay heavy, tomb-like. Horizontal light peered between shutter slats which peeled in grey, nickel-sized scabs. A sigh. Mascara smudged eyes shot open, found the room's only window. Nostrils flared at the pungent stink of urine and unwashed man. A sucking, open-mouthed snort erupted from the man whose dark head occupied the neighboring pillow.

"Oh...." The woman groaned, then clamped her lips shut and slipped silent as a snake from rumpled sheets. She rounded the foot of the bed, her fingers trailing the edge of a bookcase to steady her. Her toes tested obstructions, clothes, shoes, dampness, a pint bottle on its side. Three walls of bookcases filled with dusty, spore-plagued books sucked life from the room. At the doorless closet, the woman lifted a grey silk robe from a hook, then eased from the bedroom and gently pulled the door closed. She turned on the bathroom light, brushed her teeth, spat, winced. The pink tip of her tongue explored her teeth. The right front one gave. She tapped two aspirin from a bottle and swallowed them dry. She ran her fingers through her hair. A stranger stared back from the mirror.

Dawn reflected off white walls in the living room. She righted an overturned chair, gathered broken bits of glass from the dining table and dropped them into the pocket of her robe. An unadorned picture window framed a brilliant golden sun rising over the azure Mediterranean Sea. A neighbor's white dog scampered down the rocky terrain which fell away from the cottage. Nose to the ground, only the dog and God knew what scents and centuries he explored, perhaps even Nietzsche's wandering soles.

"Hi, boy," the woman whispered, touching the window. "I'm Sara. I offered you cheese once." Her fingertips trailed down her reflection. Far below, dark, glossy, fist-sized rocks covered the beach. A green and white fishing boat churned a milky froth wake across the teal colored bay.

Movement on the coast road caught Sara's eye. A bus on its daily run to Nice rocked back and forth as it navigated the narrow curving corniche. Just before its stop in front of the café, taillights tap-tap-tapped red. Sara touched her lip. Riders got off, riders got on, people going about their lives. Well after the bus carried on, she stared at the spot where it had been.

On her way to the kitchen, she studied the floor to avoid the ever-present stares. Seductive lips and inviting postures on walls taunted her from gaudy gold frames. Poses suggested fragrant oils and sounds and sex. Sara hurried into the kitchen, filled the tea kettle, put it on the stove, and then grabbed it before it whistled. Moments later with a small breakfast tray balanced on her palms, she nudged the back door closed with her hip.

An overgrown path led to a garden shed tucked below a decrepit out-building. She placed the tray on a metal café table on the small gravel patio, then ducked inside the shed. One window faced the sea. Below the sill sat a worm-eaten gardener's table upon which earth-soiled clay pots were stacked flush with the wall. Under the table stood a battered wooden chest scattered with an array of rusty, dented garden tools. Sara moved the tools and opened the chest. Inside were a hat box and a black leather bag. From the bag, she extracted a crinkled magazine and put it aside, then straightened and finger-pressed the lapels of a red tweed garment which had been folded and stored beneath the magazine.

Outside, she pulled an iron chair to the table, sat and then poured milk into a delicate Limoges teacup on the tray. She added sugar and steaming tea and stirred with a tiny silver spoon. Pages of the magazine flipped through her fingertips which lingered sometimes on photographs of couples with beautiful white teeth, other times on immaculate homes with well-tended gardens. She frowned, she exclaimed, she sighed. A dog-eared story required a closer look. Her lips moved. A wistful smile played on her lips. The handsome pair in the photograph wore khaki shorts, broad-brimmed straw hats, and long sleeved white shirts rolled to the elbow. They knelt on a beach beside a wire enclosure with a handwritten sign attached: Do Not Disturb Loggerhead Turtle Nest, Harbor Island, South Carolina.

Above Sara a sea gull hovered and laughed. She looked up and watched it sail toward the sea on invisible currents.

"Saaaaaraaa," a gruff male voice yelled. Muffled profanities followed. "I need you. Where the hell are you?"

Always English. French required too much effort for him. She tossed the magazine on top of the clothing in the satchel and looked around the shed. A short stack of newspapers lay in the corner. Sara wrapped the teacup, saucer, spoon and tea pot in newsprint, placed the set on top of the magazine and then grabbed the tray and hurried to the cottage.

"Finishing your breakfast, Paul," she said.

While coffee dripped, she placed two croissants on a plate with a smear of butter and two dollops of strawberry jam. Several minutes later the aroma of dark roast followed her to the bedroom. Lifting a robe from its hook, Sara held it out for the rail-thin naked man who sat on the edge of the bed. In their matching grey silks, the two looked like stick-figure twins.

Sara went to the picture window, stared at the view and listened. Paul's shoulder constricting cough broke phlegm from his tortured lungs. He hawked into the toilet then urinated.

Why wouldn't he close the door?

"Check your blood sugar while you're in there." She insisted he monitor his diabetes. Own it. It's yours, she thought.

Paul turtle-walked to the wing chair next to the picture window, then dropped into it. Breakfast awaited him on a tray on a small round wooden table.

"Coffee," Paul croaked. He took a sip, lit up a cigarette and inhaled deeply. Sara placed a Golden Gate Bridge ashtray, Paul's sole possession from home, on the table.

"Let's go to Paris." Paul coughed. Ashes sprinkled his chest from the cigarette cupped in the hand over his mouth.

Sara frowned. "I worked in a hospital there. I came here to get away from the city, remember?"

Paul's eyes closed. His lips parted, revealing stained teeth. "We met on the beach here, didn't we? Tell me about it."

Sara drew in her breath. This story was often repeated. "I had just gotten off the train from Paris. The beach looked lovely." She studied her fingernails. The cuticles were dry and needed attention. "You stared at me. I went for a swim. When I got out, I gathered my things and left." Paul drew on his cigarette. "Eat something, Paul. The bread is fresh."

While he nibbled Sara went to the kitchen and returned with a glass of water.

"You came to my gallery," Paul said, "looking for me probably. You were quite taken by an oil painting of the harbor."

"Yes," she said. But she wasn't looking for him. Something about the way he had looked at her…. "I was looking for a job when I wandered into your gallery."

"Aha. And you found one." He blew a stream of smoke. "My pretty little nurse." He got to his feet like a praying mantis with twigs for limbs and walked toward the sofa.

Sara stared out at the beautiful blue-green water. *Mon dieu.*

"Eeeahh…." Paul swept his bony knot of a fist across the coffee table. Papers and books scattered.

Sara jumped, her water spilled, her free fingertips touched the dark blue bruise throbbing on her cheek.

"I can't stand clutter." Paul's sunken chest heaved in and out. He fell onto the sofa in a jumble of angles.

Sara crossed her arms and stared at Paul's lopsided, uneven-toothed grin. Halloween's wicked jack-o-lantern.

"Let me look at you," he said as he pulled at the sash of his robe. His other hand dug between cushions and produced a glass which he sniffed, then drained of a cloudy amber liquid.

Sara's cheeks reddened. She took a deep breath, then loosened her sash. Her downcast eyes followed the grey silk as it slid down her thighs and pooled around her feet.

"Hey," Paul said.

Sara's head jerked up.

"You're my nurse. I pay you good money to take care of me." A back -heaving coughing fit threatened his lungs.

"Come." Paul's long knobby toes stretched, his boney thighs flexed. She knew what he wanted. "Come here," he said, his gravelly whisper a command.

Thirty minutes later, Sara slipped into her robe and glanced out the picture window. A pint of Scotch lay on the floor beside Paul's hand. Finding all of his hiding places had proven a futile battle. He was clever. He snored like a male bear the day after the start of mating season.

Sara tiptoed to the bathroom, cleaned her teeth and showered, long and hot. After pulling on her underthings and robe, she stuffed toiletries into a small canvas makeup kit and lingerie into a hand crocheted grocery bag. From a stack of folded clothing on her side of the closet, she pulled a leather wallet fat with cash. This she tucked in securely among her underwear.

In the kitchen Sara prepared Paul's afternoon snack tray and put it on the table beside his ignored breakfast. She slipped out the back door and retraced her steps from that morning. Inside the shed she opened the wooden chest and removed the hatbox, then opened the satchel and moved her tea things to the potting table. She shrugged off her robe and tossed it into a corner. The silk collected cobwebs as it floated to the dirt floor. From the satchel she gathered up a tweed jacket and matching skirt, leaving the magazine. She gave the clothing a shake, then stepped into the skirt and smoothed the fabric over her hips. She slipped on the jacket, carefully slipped buttons through button holes, then tugged gently on the sleeves.

From her plastic bag, she extracted a pair of resoled black leather boots and pulled them on. She flipped off the top of the hatbox and lifted out a handful of tissue paper which fluttered to the floor. She cradled a red wool beret for a moment, then placed it on her head. Sara gathered her tea set and put it gently in the satchel on top of the magazine, then she added her crocheted grocery bag. She fastened the satchel, gripped its handles with one hand while the other grabbed the canvas bag. One glance around the shed, and out the door she went.

Photo by M.Z. Thwaite

A couple in hiking shorts and boots walked the stony trail just ahead. Sara glanced back. The medieval town of Eze looked down from the pinnacle of rock above the cottage. A red bird sat on the sill of the window of the garden shed. Sara smiled, fancied herself free as that bird. The little café table and chair and her pretty flowers looked like a postcard. The pile of broken whiskey bottles in the back corner of the lot spoiled it, but she had her picture.

Sara walked on, staring at the brake lights down the hill. Her new soles crunched over small loose rocks and skittered over the hard-packed trail. The lights changed from red to out. Diesel fumes belched from the exhaust. Her feet found purchase on asphalt, and her hand grabbed the beret from her head and waved and waved and waved. Bus lights went red. Azure sea met infinite blue sky.

The bus waited.

THE BICYCLIST

Jayne Bowers

LILLIE WORE DENIM CAPRIS and a hot pink oxford shirt from the Gap. The sweltering heat from the afternoon sun hit her full in the face as she walked out of Target balancing three bags of food and toiletries. Her Rainbow Sandals slapped against her soles as she trudged towards the car.

She smiled at the memory of something a student had said to her a couple of years ago when Lillie complained about ill-fitting shoes.

The student said, "It's all about the look, Miz Lillie, all about the look."

Lillie had laughed in agreement.

And here she was again, still thinking about the look more than the comfort. Even with her sleeves rolled up, she was hot as blazes.

Geez Louise, she thought, remembering a book she'd read about Partners in Health and their work in Haiti. She had just walked out of Target with pizza, yogurt, bananas, bagels and hair color, and in Haiti, they've probably never even heard of bagels. They're starving in Cange, and she was living a fat, rich life in Myrtle Beach.

Lillie was so impressed after reading about Dr. Paul Farmer's work in Haiti, Peru and Russia she couldn't stop yakking about him to anyone who would listen.

The world needs more people like him, she thought for the umpteenth time. Lillie quickly assuaged her conscience by remembering something Dr. Farmer had said, something like, "You don't have to do what I do – just do something."

But what? she wondered, arms already tired from holding the heavy bags. And holy cow, she was burning up. How do they stand the heat in Haiti? And all those mosquitoes and flies?

Lillie glanced up, surprised to see a man on a bicycle looking at her. Tanned, handsome and in his mid to late 30's, his longish hair was wavy and brown. His clothes, including a down vest, were brown too.

As the bicyclist blocked further passage to her car, Lillie felt a tad alarmed. Who was this man, and what did he want? And why was he wearing a down vest on such a hot day? Was it all about the look for him, too?

An overstuffed duffel bag was strapped on the back of the bike. Was he homeless? Were all his worldly possessions crammed in that bag?

"Excuse me, Ma'am," he said.

Lillie thought he was staring at her turquoise necklace, a treat she had bought for herself at an art shop in Williams, Arizona, for one reason and one reason alone: she wanted it. Semi-retired and free to travel, Lillie and her husband had visited Sedona, Flagstaff, Paige, Williams and the Grand Canyon National Park.

"My fiancée and I just moved here from Kansas," the stranger said, "and we haven't been able to find work. Could you help us out a little?"

Why would a woman agree to marry a homeless man and follow him to another state?

If Lillie put the bags down to get the measly three dollars out of her purse, he'd see the yogurt, bananas, and pizza. And the money seemed like such a paltry sum. It would be embarrassing to give him three bills while she kept the three bags. But if Lillie gave him the Target purchases, then he'd have her Clairol hair color. Dilemma.

"No, I'm sorry," she said. "I can't."

If Lilly gave him the Target purchases, then he'd have her Clairol hair color. Dilemma.

"No, I'm sorry," she said. "I can't."

Balancing her bags, Lillie walked around him towards her air-conditioned car. Her shirt, likely stitched by someone laboring in a sweatshop in Bangladesh, felt damp and clingy against her skin.

Photo from Pixabay - CCO Public Domain

THE LOVERS

David Dixon

THE PHONE TRAILER DOOR OPENED and a private stepped out. "Third from the end, on the left, Sergeant," he said, then slung his rifle over his shoulder and walked off.

Hampton went inside. The trailer was, as usual, cramped and full. An aisle ran down the center, and to either side were AT&T pay phones separated by grafittied plywood partitions. Hampton made his way to the empty spot the soldier had mentioned, taking care not to trip over rifles on the floor.

He sat down in the worn plastic chair between the partitions, pulled out his AT&T card and dialed the phone number from memory.

While he listened to AT&T's inane thanks for his service and invitation to buy more minutes, he admired the graffiti – never long behind the presence of the US Army. A surprisingly good pen drawing of a large breasted woman riding Private Murphy from the *Army Times'* Murphy's Law comic made him chuckle. Finally, he put in his PIN and then his home phone number.

The phone rang, rang, and rang again. A flash of anger passed through him. This was the third time he'd tried this month, and she hadn't picked up. He let it ring.

"Hello?"

"Hey, baby, it's me – how's it going?"

"Fine, I guess."

"Okay, okay, good. I tried to call twice last week but I never got you. I was starting to – "

"I've been busy, Todd."

"Busy? So have I. I don't get to call that much, you know. What's up?"

"Huh?"

"You said you were busy, I mean, with what?"

"Stuff, you know."

"Stuff?"

"Yeah. Jason's in school, remember? I've been helping him with his homework and stuff. The car needed the oil changed. Stuff. Life doesn't stop just because you're not here, Todd."

Hampton rolled his eyes and settled back in his chair. "Okay, baby, I gotcha. I've been busy too, you know, I – "

"Yeah, I know, Todd. You're always busy." The tone was accusatory.

"What's that mean?"

"Nothing."

Hampton shook his head and swore silently to himself. "Nothing? Uh, okay, sure. Look, baby, can we just not fight, please? I haven't talked to you in two weeks, and I just want to talk, all right?"

"Fine." Hampton could picture her seven thousand miles away – sitting in the far corner on the couch, feet tucked under her, looking down at her nails. She sighed.

Hampton hated that sigh. He pressed on as if everything were indeed fine.

"So, I figure I should be back in April – looking like the fourteenth or fifteenth maybe – but April anyhow. So there's three days I'll have to stick around Killeen, and then I was thinking maybe we go up to see my mom. I'll take Jason to a game. We got a three game stand against the Cubs the twentieth through the twenty second. He'll love it. Do you think that'll work? I really don't feel like driving up there 'cause that'll take a coupla days, but if you go ahead and get three plane tickets now, it shouldn't be that bad a price – " Melanie was crying on the other end of the phone. "Melanie, what's wrong?" Her sobbing did not stop. This was not like her. What the hell was going on? "Melanie, baby, talk to me, okay? What's the matter?"

"I'm not going, Todd. You can take Jason up to see your mom if you want to but…."

"But what? What do you mean you're not going?"

"I'm not. I…I'm done, Todd. I can't do this anymore."

"Do what? The deployment? It's almost half over, goddamn it…." His voice was an angry whisper. He'd heard enough arguments in phone trailers during his deployments to know better than to shout.

"No, not the deployment. All of this – this whole thing. You and me. Us. I can't live like this."

Hampton's blood ran cold. His words came out in a flood. "Baby, baby, I know it seems bad, but like I said, it's just a little bit more, and then it's over. I'm almost done – "

"Is it, Todd? Is it really almost done? Do you expect me to believe that? It isn't almost over. You said that last time, in Afghanistan and here you are, gone again."

"Melanie, you – "

"Stop, Todd. I'm telling you, I'm done. You don't know what it does to me. You don't understand. You don't know what it's like every damn day, with Jason acting out and getting in trouble at school because – "

"You didn't tell me he was in trouble – what did he do?"

"What fucking difference would it make, Todd? You aren't here to do anything about it." Melanie's voice was thick with tears, but whether it was rage or grief, Hampton couldn't tell.

"Every day I pick him up from school," she said, "and I come home wondering whether today is the day I see one of those damn cars with two guys in Class As coming to tell us you're dead. Just – "

"How many times do I have to tell you, baby, I'm not leaving the FOB. I'm safe here, trust me." He was flustered – where was this coming from?

"*Every* day," she countered. "Last week, Nicole found out her husband lost his leg. She got home from the grocery store, and they were waiting for her. Do you know what it's like waiting and worrying every time you leave the house? That every white car you see is going to be somebody telling you your husband is not coming home? Every day I'm just waiting to find out if I'm like Nicole, or worse."

"Who's Nicole?"

"You wouldn't know, would you?" Melanie thundered. "She lives on our street – two houses down – but you're never home enough to know who lives in the neighborhood, are you? Even when you're home, you aren't home. You're out in the field, or on staff duty, or whatever else the Army has you doing. I'm surprised you even know where we live.

"I can't do it. I've had enough, Todd. We're going back to South Carolina, to Mom and Dad's. When you get back, I'll fly Jason to your mom's if you want to meet him there."

He was stunned. "Baby, I'm almost done here, okay, I –"

"No, you aren't almost done. You always say that. You've been saying that for the twelve years we've been married, and it's never true. Never has been. Never will be.

"When you get back here, you're gonna get two weeks of leave, and then you'll be back at it – either training or telling us we're gonna move again to Campbell or Bliss or wherever. And then, when you get there, you'll have to work real hard like you always do to take care of your soldiers and all that bullshit and be in the field or in California or Louisiana for training for a month, and then you'll be gone again. It is not almost done. It's about to start again.

"Hampton's mouth was dry. "Melanie, baby, you know we've got to train before – "

"Yes, I know, Todd. But what about us?" Melanie said. "What about us, huh? When are you going to take a month off from the Army to take care of us? When are….." She trailed off and broke down again.

"Baby, I've got sixteen years in. Only four more left – "

"Four more, huh? You think so? Two years of being a first sergeant where we'll never see you, and then two more where the Army will send you on another deployment, and then you'll be talking about making sergeant major and staying in even longer. I know you, Todd. Don't lie to me – four more years, my ass." She was in a rage.

"I promise, baby, I promise, I do these next four, and then I'm done, out, okay? Even if they give me sergeant major, I'll decline. Just –"

"Right." Her tone was bitter.

Hampton looked around the plywood walls, but there was no help. Instead, a soldier's grim limerick in blue pen mocked him:

Snuffy thought he had a life
Snuffy thought he had a wife.
But that bitch left him in the sand
And now Snuffy fucks his hand.

"What do you want me to do, Melanie?" His voice rose. "I'm sitting here in fuckin Iraq. I'm coming home in a coupla months. I promise – "

"I'm done," she said flatly. "I'm done with the Army. I'm done living like this. I'm not going to do it anymore."

"What do you want, Melanie? What can I do?" he pleaded.

"You can promise me you're going to be home every night, like normal people are. You can promise me you're not going to miss another anniversary or Jason's seventh birthday because you're in the field. Promise me. That's what you can do."

He closed his eyes and saw his wife and son in the darkness. "I can't promise that, baby, you know –"

"Yes, Todd, I know," she snapped. "That's why I'm leaving, can't you get that?" She sighed. "Jason and I are going back to Spartanburg in two days. We're not going to be here when you get back. I'm not taking anything but clothes and Jason's toys and my car. I'm not even taking any money out of the account except for gas – Mom and Dad will pay for everything – "

"I don't care about that. I just want my wife and son to be there when I get home."

"I know. And I just want Jason to have his daddy for his tee ball games, but sometimes we just don't get what we want."

Hampton blinked back tears. Not here. Not now. Not like this. "And how is this going to help me see Jason more, Melanie? Answer me that. This is just making things worse. Think about it, just – "

"I have, Todd. I have thought about it. I've been thinking about it for months? I made up my mind, and it isn't changing. I'm done. I am fucking done."

"Baby, Melanie, I love you – "

"No, Todd, *I* love *you. Jason* loves *you. You* love the Army or whatever this shit is."

Hampton's eyes were wet, and his mind was racing, but to where, he couldn't say.

"Todd," she continued, her voice flat and drained, "I really do love you, and I know you're a good man, but you just don't understand. You just don't get it. Me and Jason cannot keep doing this."

"Oh, please, baby… Melanie, please, at least wait until I get back. We can work it out, ju-just wait – "

"No. I can't wait because…." She broke off. "Because then you'll get me to stay, because I love you. I really do, but I can't stay, and neither can Jason. I can't wait, because then it'll just happen again, and it'll be even worse. I can't go through this anymore. I can't wait…." She wept again.

Hampton tried to swallow the lump in his throat. "I love you, baby, please – "

"Call Mom and Dad's if you want to talk to Jason. I love you, and I know you think you love me too, but it just – we can't, Todd."

"Melanie –"

"Call Mom and Dad's after this week, Todd."

"No, baby, please, no –"

"Bye, Todd."

The line went dead.

Photo by Barbara V, Evers

WHAT I SHOULD HAVE DONE

Valerie Keiser Norris

DUST SWIRLED AROUND the Honda Accord as I turned from the dirt road onto the long gravel driveway to my brother's house, built two miles from where we grew up. Rural Michigan's roads and driveways usually stayed unpaved since it made them easier to maintain during the brutal winters. As I neared the house, Dad walked head down toward me, thinner than last I'd seen him. He wore only a pair of dark shorts.

Melanoma last year, and now he's shirtless in the July sun?

My sister-in-law, Patty, ran to catch up with Dad and helped him pull on a shirt. Her mouth moved, but with the car's windows up I heard nothing. She pulled his arm and turned him back toward the house.

Neither paid attention to my approach, although I'd just driven seven hundred miles to visit.

Closer now, I realized the thin, nearly bald man was too tall to be Dad.

My brother, Warren, post brain-tumor surgery.

He'd visited me in South Carolina just three months ago, misdiagnosed with vertigo, and at that time he'd looked older and more tired than he had when I'd seen him last summer. Since then he'd aged years.

Patty and Warren disappeared into the open garage without a backward glance. I stopped near the other four vehicles already parked in the driveway.

My younger sister, Joy, came from behind the house as I stepped out of the car.

"Alice," she said. Lean, strong, the picture of health, Joy held a large basket of vegetables with both hands. She dropped the basket, vegetables spilling, and ran and threw her slim arms around me. "Thank God you're here." Her voice came out airy, choked.

"I'm sorry. I couldn't get away." Three weeks ago Warren's "vertigo" had finally been diagnosed as an aggressive brain tumor, and surgery followed within a week.

Ever since Mom's death, I felt the need to mother my younger siblings. It never occurred to me I might need to mother my older brother.

I should have been here.

Joy pulled away and wiped at her eyes with the backs of her hands. "Sorry. I was fine till I saw you. I'm just glad you're here now. It's – bad." She turned to the basket she'd dropped.

We gathered the fallen tomatoes and green beans, yellowed cucumbers and overgrown zucchini from Warren's beloved garden, then I followed her toward the garage side door.

"I just saw Warren and Patty in the driveway, but they didn't notice me," I said.

Joy shook her head. "It's not a good day."

My throat clenched. "Everyone kept telling me things were going okay."

"They were. Now they're not." She led the way into the ranch-style house.

I should have been here.

Warren met me in the kitchen with a hug and a smile, but no words. Deep scratches laced his arms and legs. His hair had thinned over the years. Now the shaved section of scalp highlighted the scar charting the side of his head.

My sister-in-law, Patty, greeted me with a tired smile. "How was your trip? Can I get you anything?"

"Go take a nap," Joy told her. "I'll take care of things."

Patty excused herself. Joy asked Warren how he was, if he was tired, did he need something to drink, did he need to use the bathroom.

Did he need to use the bathroom? I felt as if I'd dropped into the middle of someone else's life.

"Walk," he said.

"Okay, let's walk." She took his arm and opened the door that led back to the garage. Over her shoulder, she said, "Dad and Nick are out on the deck."

I poured myself a glass of water and headed for the deck. Dad and my younger brother, Nick, who lived nearby, sat on white resin chairs, empty beer cans on the table between them.

Dad glanced up. "Hi, honey. What's Warren doing?"

"He and Joy are taking a walk." I hadn't seen Dad or Nick in a year, but they acted as if my presence was nothing unusual.

Maybe because everything was unusual.

No longer arm in arm, Joy and Warren passed below the deck across the grassy back yard. Joy waved. Warren paced steadily, concentrating on the ground.

"I'm glad Joy's taking this go-round," Dad said. "He wore me out earlier."

"He walks a lot?"

Nick nodded. "It's like a compulsion. He walks in a pattern around the yard, around and around. One time his path included opening his truck door, sliding across the seat, and out the other door."

As Joy and Warren paced around the house again, Nick filled me in on all they'd kept from me. Warren's night wandering. Arranging fishing lures in the main living areas of the house. Waking Patty at 3:00 AM, frantic to find that man, the man who promised to take them to church and pray. The man who turned out to be TV's Dr. Oz. Yesterday Warren had slipped out of the house. Someone three miles away called the police about a scratched and bloody old man who appeared "not right."

Joy and Warren lapped the house again.

Warren and I were born eleven months apart, *Irish twins*, people called us. As a child, when my December birthday came I'd sing-song, "I'm as old as you are." When we got older, he'd call me and tease, "You're as old as I am."

Would he be here this December?

Dad's brother and his wife arrived a half an hour later, and we moved to the garage to get out of the sun. Webbed lawn chairs surrounded a card table, an ashtray filled with cigar butts the only decoration. Dad and Nick found drinks for everyone and joined my aunt and uncle at the table. Warren sat with them and lit up a cigar. Joy and I perched about eight feet away on the step into the kitchen.

"Finally done walking?" I said.

"Yep. I asked if he was ready to stop. He thought about it and said, 'One more,' so we did one more and then he could stop." She swiped her damp forehead with the back of her freckled arm.

Beaming at everyone around the table, Warren occasionally tossed in comments that had nothing to do with the conversation: "My son is coming." "My sisters are here."

"I didn't know – " I choked.

Joy put her arms around me and patted my shoulder. "It hasn't been this bad the whole time. Surgery couldn't get the entire tumor. What we're seeing could be from the tumor or the steroids. They don't know."

I should have been here.

She got up to start spaghetti sauce for supper, declining my offer to help.

Warren rose. Nick and Dad leaned forward. "Where are you going?" they both said.

Pointing in my direction, he came and sat beside me on the step. He opened his mouth, and a frown wrinkled his brow. He tried again, but still no words came forth.

"I know you're having problems with speech," I said. "It must be frustrating. Just try to be patient with us. We'll figure out what you're trying to say."

Hands clasped between his knees, his scratches still red and angry, he looked at me but didn't respond. Then his head, his scarred, half-bald head, tipped toward me, and he leaned against me. We sat, head touching head, for a long moment.

Then he bolted out of the garage and down the driveway. Nick ran to join him.

I should have been here.

MARTIN GETS A LETTER

Ferguson Williams

IT WAS OFFICIAL. Martin McClintock was scheduled for recall. Recall was his name for it. He'd also heard revoke, the big take back, shit outta luck (that was the sinners' special), and the Rapture. That was a favorite of the bible thumpers. Whatever it was called didn't matter though. His number was up, and he knew it as soon as he opened his mailbox.

His letter, which from what he'd seen on the news and heard about town was the customary way of notification, arrived on a Tuesday. No trumpets. No fanfare. Just as unassuming as any bit of junk mail. There was no way anyone other than Martin would know what it was unless they read his mail, and that was a crime. He, however, knew immediately.

There was no return address, no postage stamp, and no postmark cancellation indicating that the letter had been places in order to get to him. There was only his name handwritten in flowing penmanship. The script was lovely and light, almost like a lover had written it to discuss something trivial, whimsical, like a recent visit or a party, not a man's death.

No, Martin, not death, he reminded himself. On the news, scientists and psychologists and anyone else calling themselves experts said it wasn't death because there were no bodies found or anything to confirm that anyone was technically dead. The people just weren't there anymore. Instead, the know-it-alls called it Supernatural Evanesce and swore up and down that one day, under correct conditions, those people might return. Martin McClintock called that horseshit. Not a single solitary person had returned since this whole thing started. Not one.

Photo from Pixabay - CCO Public Domain

Martin had been on the porch thumbing through *The Sun News*, perusing the list of letter recipients the newspaper had taken to printing every day. Some days the register was short; others sometimes were so long the list continued on another page. Mr. so and so. Mrs. who's -it. Date of birth. Age. Date of receipt. Sometimes other family members' names were listed as well under the heading "remembered in the physical by…." The whole thing was morbid and black, like staring at a car crash expecting to see dead bodies, but it had become a part of life, second nature.

August 20. There were six today.

He put the paper down when he realized the mail had come.

His letter was right on top. He was taken aback for a moment. Then he found himself frantically searching for the mailman who had rolled in his motorized buggy to the next house. Because there were no other houses beyond that one, the vehicle turned around and traveled up the opposite side of the street. Martin waited for it to pass, waited to see if perhaps the deliverer of his finality was a demonic beast or an angelic being, but it was neither.

It was Raul, the same kid who always delivered the mail. The same kid whose merengue music spilled out of his headphones when he brought large envelopes or packages up the walk to the front door. The same kid who stalled at the gate, then came up and offered his condolences when Martin's daughter, Shelly, had gone missing.

Raul smiled and waved. Martin returned both gestures. Then he realized that where Raul had a purpose, to deliver the rest of the mail, he suddenly had nothing. What exactly was he supposed to be doing, to be feeling, now that he was certain he had received his walking papers? Walking papers? Martin was sure he'd never heard that one before.

Going back to his newspaper seemed futile. Soon enough someone would be reading his name in print in the same fashion. "Make sure it is what you think it is, before you go all dust in the wind, Martin," he whispered. Dust in the wind? He chuckled. "I should be writing these down."

Opening the letter in the yard seemed wrong, like exposing himself in public, so he decided to escape to his tool shed off the side of the house. He had meant to paint the old shack years ago but things always seemed to come up: the car needed repairs or the playoffs or the search for Shelly. Always something.

He slid the wooden door open, walked past the paints, the lawn mower, the Weedwacker and sat at the work bench in the back. Dust preserved tinkerings he hadn't touched in years. This used to be his favorite spot, a kind of watering hole for him and his male neighbors. They used to exchange tools and talk shop and shoot the shit, but it had been a while since any of them were anything more to him than hi and bye.

On the shelf in front of him sat a plethora of junk and a brown wooden box engraved with the words *The End of the World*. At the time of naming the box he was trying to be funny, not thinking there would be an end, at least not one that he would see coming. Inside was a petrified joint, an Air Force emblazoned Zippo and a mini bottle of Wild Turkey.

The off-white envelope sat on his lap like a Bible. For a moment he contemplated not opening it at all, letting the chips fall where they may, so to speak. What could possibly come from knowing? But then he remembered a story on CNN about a man in New York who was beaten to death by an unknown group of assailants.

"Assholes is more like it," Martin had told his wife Susan. When they searched the man's belongings, the police found his still sealed letter. His date was March 24. He died March 25. No way in hell that was a coincidence. And there were other stories just like that. People who didn't open their letters or tried to outsmart the recall and the result was violent, swift.

Martin had to open it.

Heavy and crisp like résumé paper, folded neatly in three sections, there was only a date hand written in the middle of the page. August 28. "And this will be the day that I die," he sang out. He imagined he should be upset, angry, something about his recall, but he wasn't.

The people he'd seen on TV who got their letters were either devastated or rejoicing. He'd only seen one man, a gray haired gentleman from down South, who seemed to mirror Martin's feelings. When asked by a reporter what he thought after he got his letter, the man simply replied, "It is what it is."

"It is what it is," Martin repeated and reached for *The End of the World*.

A few hours later, Martin sat at his dining room table with a bucket of fried chicken Susan had picked up on her way home from work. She was complaining about some woman from the office when he, mid-chicken breast, began giggling uncontrollably. Susan paused her story and stared at him. She couldn't help but chuckle as well, although she looked unsure as to what they were laughing about.

"Shelly the vegan," he replied to her questioning expression. He snatched his napkin from his lap and wiped the jubilant tears that pooled in the corners of his eyes.

Susan smiled at the memory. "Yeah, all because of that smelly, greasy Earth Day boy she met that summer. Remember, he would only wash once a month and wore that all-natural deodorant?" She put a fork full of mashed potatoes in her mouth, and shook her head.

"Yeah, Onion Spice," he chuckled. This time the tears fell unopposed.

Susan suddenly laughed, showing a mouth full of white that she quickly covered with her napkin.

"Re-remember we had steaks for dinner that one night, and he gave us that speech about how we were eating once living creatures abused for human consumption?" Martin said it with the same haughtiness that Onion Spice had used.

"He wouldn't eat, and neither would she," Susan added, grinning ear to ear.

"An-and remember we thought we heard a burglar that night, but… but," he could hardly contain himself to finish the story, "it was her sitting on the kitchen floor, eating cold steak in the dark like an animal. The three of us screamed so loud when you flicked the lights on that the neighbors called the police."

Susan laughed with such vigor she almost fell out of her chair. He loved seeing her like this, happy, tossing back her blonde locks peppered with gray a little sooner than they should have been. In this moment she looked so much like the daughter they hadn't seen in years.

The sounds of cheerfulness gradually subsided, and then a more familiar Susan reappeared. "I miss her so much." She sighed as if the pain was fresh, new. "Do you think she was recalled too?" She'd probably been holding on to that glimmer of hope since this whole Supernatural Evanesce thing started. But Shelly had left long before that.

She always wandered back home though, usually with a story to tell or a new boyfriend or the last time with a drug addiction her parents wondered if she'd had all along. She was a free spirit. They had somewhat accepted that, but it'd been seven years now. Not a word from her. She was dead, not "one day she'll return" dead like the people on TV said. Martin knew in his heart she was dead. Dead like "buried with her their hopes and dreams of graduations, story book weddings, and grandchildren" dead.

"I just don't understand why she won't just come home," Susan said.

Martin nodded. Gazing at his coleslaw, he felt guilt. He wasn't sure why, maybe it was the weed he'd smoked earlier or maybe it was because he would be one more person to leave his wife without a real explanation.

Susan stared into her plate and swirled peas around with her plastic spork.

"Remember," she said, "that time she wanted to be Goth so bad she used that black Sharpie on her lips and got that terrible rash?"

And the two of them laughed again so joyfully Martin decided tomorrow would be a better day to tell his wife the time was coming when he wouldn't come home again either.

Photo by Jayne Bowers

TAKING CARE OF DADDY

Bob Strother

TYLER STOOD IN THE DOORWAY like a sentinel, still and watchful, waiting for the sound of silence – or, if he were completely truthful with himself – praying for it. Seconds dragged by. He checked his watch. Nearly half a minute had passed. A tingling sensation crept up his shins, wound around his hips and fanned out over his shoulders. His ears picked up the soft chuff of the spinning clothes dryer, the persistent insectile buzz of the fluorescent light over the kitchen sink, but nothing else. Then, just as the first needle of adrenalin pierced his quickening heart, a raspy intake of breath signaled his father was still among the living.

He sighed, turned from his spot just near the bedroom and walked into the adjacent living room. Outside, a late October breeze sent dry leaves scuttling across the yard. The afternoon was cloudy, heavy with the portent of rain. Tyler sat on the threadbare loveseat, his back to the window, and riffled listlessly through the array of reading material he'd brought. Before, he might read a novel every three or four weeks. Now, here in the home he'd grown up in years ago, he'd knock out one or two over the weekend – *his* weekend. Since his father's stroke, he and his three brothers each took one weekend a month caring for him.

Caring for him. Now there was a word with all sorts of connotations. They'd all been deeply concerned at the outset, but optimistic for at least some degree of physical rehabilitation. At eighty-three, his father had been healthy and active, still working when he had the opportunity. Even before the stroke, however, Tyler and his siblings had watched their father's small but consistent plumbing supply business slip helplessly into the churning maw of progress. Lowe's and Home Depot had taken their toll. It hadn't been a real problem for each of the brothers to toss in a couple of hundred bucks a month to help out with living expenses. But now, twenty-six weeks after the stroke, the old man completely bedridden and seldom conscious, it was a different story. Concern for their father had quickly been eclipsed by concern over the staggering outlay of funds required for his home care.

They'd eased the burden by splitting the weekend responsibilities, but around the clock weekday care still amounted to almost a thousand a week. Nursing homes were even more expensive, and neither he nor his brothers were wealthy. They'd worked hard to put enough aside for retirement, and now, as in the Paul Simon song, they saw it all slip-sliding away.

The backdoor opened with a familiar squeak. Tyler glanced up. Morgan entered through the kitchen and peeked around the corner. Morgan was the youngest brother, and the only one yet to retire.

"What's up, bro?" Morgan said.

"Same old stuff."

Morgan stole a glance toward his father's bedroom. "Any change?"

"He sleeps, wakes up enough to eat a bite or two occasionally, then sleeps again."

"Thought I'd stop by for a minute and take a quick peek."

"Be my guest." Tyler followed Morgan into the bedroom.

Morgan crossed his arms over his chest, looking down on the sleeping figure for several minutes, then blew out a long breath and shrugged. The two brothers stepped back into the living room.

"Jesus," Morgan said, "he looks like death on a cracker."

"That's what you said a month ago."

"Still true, though."

They were quiet for a moment, gazing out through the bay window their father had installed three decades earlier. A plastic grocery bag hung from the lower branch of a leafless maple, snapping in the breeze like a stadium pennant. Then Morgan said, "I don't know how long I can keep shelling out this kind of money, bro."

"I know," Tyler replied. "We're all hurting." It was true. First, the economic meltdown had slashed through his and his brothers' 401Ks like a scythe, then this.

Morgan turned and stared at the wall where a family portrait hung, a testament to happier times. "Mom went so quickly, smiling and happy one day, gone the next."

"Aneurysms are like that, I guess. Stroke victims tend to linger."

"But he looks so damn bad," Morgan said.

Tyler placed a hand on his brother's shoulder. "The nurse says his vital signs are stable enough."

Morgan took another deep breath and let it out. "I wish … I wish … I mean he can't enjoy being like this, can he?"

I know what you wish, Tyler thought. I think we're all hoping for the same thing. We just don't give voice to it. "I don't believe he enjoys anything at this point. He barely knows where he is, if that."

"I need to go," Morgan said. "I'll just look in on him one more time before I do."

Tyler nodded and went into the kitchen for a cup of coffee. He added sugar and was searching for the creamer when he sensed Morgan behind him.

"I think he's crapped in his diaper," Morgan said.

"I'll take care of it." Tyler sipped his coffee and watched his brother leave.

Morgan was correct. The stench was pungent and hung heavily over the hospital-style bed. Tyler lifted off the bedcovers, unfastened the Velcro strips of the soiled diaper, and grimaced as he folded it back. He had never in his life thought he'd become so familiar with his father's nether regions.

When he was through with the cleanup, he sprayed the room with deodorizer and tucked the sheet and blanket back around the old man's shoulders. It was like dealing with a life-size, dead weight mannequin, swiveling the appendages, propping them up, straightening them out. Not once had his father roused, even with all the manipulations.

Tyler checked his watch again, counted the seconds between breaths, waited. He picked up one of the pillows he'd used to prop his father's legs while he'd cleaned him, and held it pressed to his chest. Then, after a while, he tucked it back against the bed rail, and returned to the living room.

He found himself surrounded by complex and contradictory emotions, like bats at dusk swooping down from different directions. He turned on the radio for distraction, realized it was tuned to a Christian rock station, and turned it off again. He'd never liked that kind of music, felt it was bad for both God and rock and roll.

The disturbing thoughts he'd had earlier stayed with him. He wondered if his brothers experienced the same thing. His gaze wandered, finally coming to rest on the floor-to-ceiling bookshelf where a scuffed baseball sat between the *American Heritage Dictionary* and a stack of *National Geographic* magazines. Tyler walked over and retrieved it, fingering the smooth white leather and the ribbed red stitching – a leftover prize from his high school days. He remembered the sharp ping of the bat, running flat-out to snag fly balls, his dad in the bleachers cheering him on.

Thunder rumbled, shaking the house, and fat pellets of rain splatted against the bay window, steady and loud. Like God was pitching sidearm.

It would be so easy, Tyler thought. No one would be suspicious. Even the weekday caregivers speculated openly on the inevitability of his father's passing. It would make everything so much less complicated.

He could do it – probably with his siblings' unspoken blessing. Then he pictured again his father's hug after Tyler's team won the regional baseball championship, the beard stubble rough against his cheek, the unlikely kiss planted on his forehead. Sometimes, he thought, it's the little things that make the difference, the road paved by degrees, a thousand paths taken or not. Take your eye off the road, and you hit a cement truck or cream a nun in a crosswalk. But the little things kept finding their way into the equation. Something here – a word or gesture or action – prevents something there.

And, Tyler figured, there was a world of difference between a thought and an action. One was written on the wind, the other carved in stone. He could help his father on to the great beyond, whatever that might be, and everyone would be quietly happy and relieved that the outflow of funds would be staunched.

He rolled the baseball between his palms – one of the little things. Yeah, he could do it. But he wouldn't.

Not *this* weekend, anyway.

Photo by Edith Hawkins

CREATIVE

NONFICTION

Photo by Edith Hawkins

WAITING ROOM

M.B. Gibson

I SIT IN A CENTRAL FLORIDA mental health facility, listening to a pair of cops discuss the painting behind me. The one decorative piece in the institutional waiting room depicts a marina in Monte Carlo. The officers smile as they lean against the take-in window, debating the virtues of a Mediterranean vacation. The artwork, I suppose, is designed to be calming.

A young man and I politely nod, but do not join the conversation. I assume he is waiting for a family member as I am, but when the door to the restricted part of the facility buzzes, the policemen take the guy back.

I'm scared. My daughter is behind that locked door completing the bureaucratic paperwork required to hospitalize her husband, Patrick, against his will.

I love Patrick. He and my daughter, Felicia, have been together ten years, married for four. He's brilliant, interesting and funny. The two of us have shared many lively conversations, some lasting hours.

After a stint in the military, he had attended college with a double major, excelling at every turn. I was not shocked, however, when his behavior became erratic at the beginning of his senior year. We all knew there were mental health issues in his family. Ours, too, for that matter.

No worries. With proper medication and counseling, he would live a stable, happy life. I know people who do.

Those people, however, acknowledge their problem and accept help. But not here. Patrick, when healthier, alluded to the possibility of a bipolar condition, but now he denies it.

It started when he railed that Felicia didn't care about him, which escalated to shunning her, followed by emotional, if not physical, infidelity. From time to time, he'd stare off as though listening to voices. When Felicia asked what he was looking at, he'd erupt into eerie laughter and call her crazy. He once disappeared for a week, then moved to the spare room and barricaded the door to prevent her from murdering him in his sleep.

My daughter, a medical professional, read every book and article she could find. She found her own therapist and joined both online and in-person support groups. When Felicia explained Patrick's behavior to her therapist, the counselor instructed her to go to the courthouse immediately. Hospitalization, she insisted, was crucial.

"This is your last chance to save your husband," she told my daughter.

The judge quickly approved the action, but a holiday weekend delayed the execution of his orders. We waited four days in anguish.

"What if he hates me forever?" Felicia asked me.

"That's a chance you have to take," I said.

At last, my daughter got the call. "We're picking him up this afternoon," the officer told her.

As planned, I drove three hundred miles to offer them both my support. Between the torrential Florida rains and my tears, it was a wonder I could see to drive. I imagined the pain in Patrick's eyes as the police ordered him into their car, his heart crumbling at the "betrayal." It had been unbearable.

In the waiting room, my heart is pounding. What's taking so long? Are they getting all the details? Will they allow her to see him?

The door opens, and Felicia steps into the reception area. I leap from my chair at the sight of her red, puffy face. The most even-keeled of my three daughters is a blubbering mess.

"What happened?" I say.

A plump woman in her late forties pokes her head through the door. "I didn't make her cry," she says.

What a curious thing to say. I look from one to the other. Felicia averts her eyes and gathers her things.

"Tell your mother I didn't make you cry," the woman repeats. Felicia grunts.

I go to the woman who identifies herself as Patrick's social worker. "What's going on?"

The social worker nods toward Felicia. "She'll tell you," she says, then pops back and closes the door.

My heartbeat throbs in my ears. I'm at a loss. What should I do?

"Let's go," my daughter says.

In the car, she explains that the social worker came into a meeting room and announced that she and a psychiatrist had spoken to Patrick, who seemed perfectly rational. However, Felicia's account in her court report shows she is paranoid.

"What?" I am stunned. Felicia's sobs erupt from an agonizing depth. This cannot be happening.

"They're going to release him today."

"They can't do that," I say. "They're allowed to keep him seventy-two hours. It's only been one night."

"He told them he wants a divorce," Felicia says. "He claims I'm only doing this to prevent that."

"And they believe him?" I am flabbergasted. "Your therapist recommended you do this. Did you tell them that?"

She nods. "It made no difference."

I curb my rising panic, as it will only make things worse. The so-called professionals are buying into the narrative Patrick has spouted for months: Communication with Felicia is causing any mental torment he suffers. He must not speak to her because she is the "crazy" one. Divorce is the only answer. Yet, he has no job, and is not searching for one. He works out, is teaching himself German and plays video games.

I swallow screams that fester in my throat. I want to run inside the hospital and ram someone against a wall. "A man's life is at stake, and you want to let him go? What kind of people are you?"

However, I am here to support, not become the problem.

Felicia relays one outrage after another. When she handed the woman a journal in which she'd detailed Patrick's unstable behaviors, the social worker threw it back at Felicia unread. "Stop writing novels and get on with your life," she snapped.

The woman rolled her eyes at each new symptom Felicia described, responding, "Some people like their voices," referring to the ones in his head. Or, "Patrick was just kidding when he did that."

She even said, "If everything you wrote on this court order were true, you'd have left a long time ago."

The psychiatrist brought Patrick to the meeting room. He sat across from his hysterical wife, emotionless. Not even when, in frustration, the even-tempered Felicia screamed, "I need a fucking Xanax," did he blink an eye. No anger, no sadness, no mockery, nothing.

"Why wasn't his robotic behavior a red flag?" I wonder aloud.

After the psychiatrist and Patrick left, Felicia realized she could not convince them of their – what, naiveté? Ignorance? Apathy? "When should I pick him up?" she said.

"Pick him up?" the woman said. "Just put him in a cab."

I, too, am frustrated and afraid. What will happen to Patrick now? Can we just give up? "Would you mind if I go in and try to talk to her?" I ask Felicia. She shakes her head.

I see myself as someone who can communicate in a calm, rational way. I will convince these people to take Felicia seriously. She's not some spurned woman who's concocted a cruel scheme worthy of an episode of *Desperate Housewives*.

Back in the waiting room I explain to the blonde woman behind the take-in window that I don't want to cause any trouble, but I must see the social worker.

The woman looks nervous. "She's in a meeting now. With another patient."

"How long does that usually take?"

"Probably thirty minutes."

"I'll wait."

As I take my old seat under the painting, the woman places a call. Somehow, within five minutes, the social worker has wrapped up her meeting. She joins me in the tiny room and sits catty-corner from me in the plastic chairs, adopting what she must think is her compassionate look. All I see is annoyance.

"First," I tell her, "in our family, we don't put people in cabs. We pick them up." I go on to explain Felicia's character and the struggle she's had with Patrick. I use my most reasonable tone, determined to change the aggravation in her eyes to genuine understanding.

She nods, then responds as though I haven't spoken. "Your job," she says, "is to take care of Felicia. I'm more worried about her than Patrick."

I fight like hell to keep from rocketing out of my chair. "Felicia will be fine. She is a strong woman with a large support system. We're all watching out for her. What about Patrick? Who's watching out for him?"

The woman actually grinned. "We have him. He's here."

"You're letting him go this afternoon."

"Well, that hasn't been decided yet."

I take a breath. Don't blow this. There's still hope. But it is short-lived.

"You know how they say your taste buds change every seven years?" she says.

"I've heard that."

"Well, your personality changes every seven years, too. Patrick's new personality just doesn't want to be with Felicia."

She's citing crazy old wives' tales now? It's clear we're just talking past each other. Yet, as long as there's a chance they may do something for Patrick, I don't want to piss her off.

"Look, you don't know me," I say, "and you don't know Felicia."

She interrupts. "Yes, I do. I see people exactly like you every day. People who care about their family members."

No, you don't, and it's clear you don't want to. Obviously, she lumps everyone into a category, and nothing will alter the stereotypical roles she's assigned us. Dejected, I thank her for her time and leave.

Back at Felicia's apartment, the social worker calls to inform us Patrick will spend one more night at the hospital "in order to give you both a chance to calm down." She will call when he is released.

But she doesn't. Patrick calls. Felicia listens, then distraught, thrusts the phone at me. In a voice devoid of emotion, which I can only assume is the one he used at the hospital, he asks that we both leave the apartment for an hour so he can gather his things.

"Certainly," I tell him. "But do you need a ride? I'll come get you."

"I have a ride." He repeats his initial request that we leave.

"But can I see you?"

"No. I just need you both to leave so I…."

Ugh. "We will. You don't *want* to see me?"

"It's not that." He says nothing more.

I agree to leave and hang up.

We quickly collect our purses and drive out of the apartment complex. Felicia is sobbing. My heart is crushed.

Apparently, he called his brother from the hospital, and we assume he is going there. The social worker never calls.

Over the next months, we hear nothing until Felicia receives an email from his lawyer. He's pursuing the divorce. My daughter concludes the pain is greater than their potential for happiness, so she is moving on.

As for Patrick, is he happy? Is he lonely? Is he well? I don't know. I still love him and I'm still waiting.

Photo by Jayne Bowers

SALAD DAYS

Bob Strother

IN HIS TRAGEDY, *Antony and Cleopatra*, Shakespeare coined the term "salad days" – a time youthful, enthusiastic, raw, and indiscrete. At seventy years of age, those days for me are long gone, but not always forgotten.

Not long ago, my wife, Vicki, tossed me a copy of Greenville's *Town Magazine* and said, "This has some interesting stuff in it. You might want to take a look."

I don't read periodicals for fear I might accidentally improve my mind, but if Vicki suggests one, I will, in the interest of matrimonial harmony, give it a glance. The theme of the issue was Southern culture, and nestled among glossy, high-dollar advertisements I discovered a photograph and an article on the long-since demolished Greenville Memorial Auditorium.

The Big Brown Box, as it was known in its own salad days, hosted some of the biggest names in entertainment: Joe Cocker, Peter Paul and Mary, Linda Ronstadt, and, in October of 1977, Lynyrd Skynyrd's final performance before their plane crashed into a Louisiana bayou.

I attended the Skynyrd concert that night with my girlfriend Sally, a twenty-seven-year- old high school teacher who lived in my Eastside singles-only apartment complex. We'd dated for about six months. I use the term "girlfriend" loosely, because I was recently divorced at the time and determined to enjoy what the band would have termed being "free as a bird." Sally exuded sweet Southern charm, had a trim, athletic body. I genuinely liked her. Why wouldn't I? She cooked frequent meals for me, bought expensive gin to complement my Schweppes, freely shared her life and her bed, and she had Cinemax.

I tried to be discrete in my trespasses against our relationship, but wasn't always successful. Like the Saturday morning when a recent catch came pounding on Sally's apartment door. I peeked carefully out her bedroom window and said, "It's someone I once had a relationship with."

"Why is she here?" Sally said.

"I broke it off. She didn't want to let go."

"How'd she know where to find you?"

"She's probably stalking me."

Later that evening, over steaks and sautéed mushrooms, we laughed about the "crazy girl" from my distant past. Bullet dodged.

Another point of contention occurred when my straying interfered with our weekend dating. My downstairs neighbor, whom I'd been secretly seeing for a few weeks, had tickets to the movie premier of *Heaven Can Wait* on a Friday night. By this time, Sally suspected our relationship was not altogether exclusive. I called to tell her I wouldn't be available for our usual Friday night meal and movie.

She breathed hurt and anger into the phone. "I thought I at least had the weekends," she said between sobs.

And so it went for a few more months until Sally finally had enough and slept with her next door neighbor in retaliation. When she told me about it, I was shocked and hurt. Hurt? Why would I hurt? Maybe I loved her after all. Certainly it felt that way at the moment. So that's what I told her. I suppose, from Sally's perspective, she'd accomplished her mission, and for the next few months, we were happy enough as a couple. But, while I had left the chase, it had not left me, and before long I reverted to my old ways.

This time, though, I really did fall in love.

I broke up with Sally on a Sunday morning. It wasn't pretty. In fact, it was a mess. She cried and screamed at me, her pretty face scrunched up in ugly lines, like a thwarted toddler. I felt bad and guilty for a while, but I had a new love to ease my discomfort.

I saw Sally twice more in the ensuing years. The first time she glared at me and said, "Do I know you?" The second time she acted as if I weren't there at all.

Hurt, anger, and love oftentimes intertwine. And then something happens that you can't forgive. You drag it around with you and remember it at odd moments, and no matter how old you get, that one thing still retains its fresh and vital pain. It's possible that's how Sally felt about my cheating and our breakup. But assuming that would be self-serving and arrogant. Probably she had moved on long ago and never thinks about me or our time together at all.

I'm now well beyond those exciting, but callous years. Age doesn't always impart wisdom, but it does, at least, give one pause. In Shakespeare's *Antony and Cleopatra* the queen laments her youthful dalliances with Julius Caesar when she says, "My salad days, when I was green in judgment, cold in blood."

The queen and I are alike – both of us hoping to be forgiven the indiscretions of our youth.

Photo by Edith Hawkins

BULLSEYE

Barbara V. Evers

WHEN I MARRIED my husband-the-deputy over twenty years ago, he told me, "I need to take you to the shooting range, so you know how to shoot the guns." I hadn't shot a gun in fifteen years, and even then it was only once, so I agreed and waited for this to happen.

A second marriage for both of us, our days filled up with the activities of two teenagers living with us and three younger children visiting on a regular basis. The guns remained secured on a top shelf of his closet. Out of sight, out of mind.

Then, we moved to a house in the country.

Last year, while discussing weekend plans, I suggested he take me to the shooting range.

"No," Bruce said, "I don't have time to make arrangements to do that."

"Like what arrangements?" I said.

"I need to buy ammo."

He had just gone through night shooting exercises which meant he had just cleaned his guns. I think he probably didn't want to clean them again.

As time passed, I kept pressing him to take me to the shooting range. "Now that we live in the country, I'd feel safer if I knew how to use the guns."

Nothing happened.

Then our dog, Abraham, died, so I no longer had his large, barking presence to protect me. When Bruce was out of town for work, I felt alone and vulnerable.

When he asked for my Christmas list, I said, "Take me to the shooting range and teach me how to use the guns. That's what I want."

Bruce appeared to consider this suggestion. "Do you want your own gun?"

The question surprised me. I never felt an overwhelming desire to own guns, although I wouldn't mind a crossbow or compound bow, since I enjoy archery. "I don't know. Not until I shoot your guns."

Christmas came. He gave me a sound board.

I dropped obvious hints.

"We can go shoot any time." he said.

"But we don't." I said.

Valentine's Day came. He gave me jewelry.

Our anniversary arrived. He gave me flowers and candy, then hugged me. "I thought we'd go look at shoes."

"I do need new shoes."

"Well, we can do that if you'd rather," he said, stepping back.

"Wait? What did you say?" What had I missed?

"I said we could go shoot, but if you'd rather get shoes, we can do that."

"Oh no. You're taking me to shoot," I told him. No way was he going to dodge this again.

So finally, we went to the shooting range.

As we filled out the release form, I caught Bruce checking his watch for the date. "Really?" I said, laughing. "Really? You had to look?"

The older man behind the counter said, "It must be your anniversary."

Bruce checked the date on his watch out of habit, but that didn't stop me from ribbing him a little about it. All right, a lot. I teased him so much that right before we went into the range, the clerk said, "I don't want any bloodshed in there, you two."

We laughed, donned our safety gear and entered the range, silhouette target in hand.

I tried the .38 revolver first, liking how easy it was to load and fire. My aim remained good, just like it had been that one time many years ago. I felt pride over hitting the center of the silhouette even though it felt weird shooting at the shape of a man.

Then I tried a SIG .380 pistol. The lady behind the gun counter told me a lot of women liked the grip on this gun. I struggled loading the clip, but once we got it loaded, I was ready to shoot and sighted for the target.

As I started to pull the trigger, Bruce said, "Pull back slowly."

I shifted my focus on my index finger, attempting a steady, but slow, pull.

When the gun fired, I felt a sharp stab. "Ow." Blood oozed from a gash on my left thumb.

"What did you do?" Bruce said.

We both stared at the blood.

"I don't know." I handed him the gun. "The slide caught my thumb somehow. It's jammed." I looked around for a tissue.

He cleared the jammed shell. "Are you OK?"

"I'm fine. Just a little blood. Let me try again."

He aimed the gun toward the target to demonstrate. "Keep your thumb down like this."

I studied what he did and realized I must have moved my thumb when I changed my focus on drawing the trigger back slowly. He handed the gun back to me, but I couldn't summon the force to reload the chamber. Blood trickled down my hand. Big blotches stained the hem of my shirt and puddled on the floor. "I think I'm going to need to clean this up."

I gave Bruce the SIG and headed out of the shooting range, the clerk's joking comment ringing in my ears: "No bloodshed."

Laughing, I approached the counter, right palm cupped to catch the blood. "Um, I need to clean this up."

To his credit, the man did not comment on my situation. He assisted me in cleaning my hand, provided multiple bandages, and when I couldn't open the bandage, did that, too.

I headed back toward the range.

"Don't forget to keep your thumb down," he called after me.

Like I'll ever forget that again.

I went back and shot the revolver, the SIG, and Bruce's 9mm. My thumb ached, but I soldiered on, determined not to give Bruce a reason to regret this trip.

As we left, I examined the stains on my clothes. I looked like I had come out of a war zone. Scattered blood stains covered my shirt. Even my sleeves carried the evidence of my anniversary gift.

On the ride home, I considered my next Facebook post: "For our anniversary, Bruce took me to the shooting range. I didn't bleed much."

HIGH AND FAR AND WIDE

Bob Strother

I MET MY FATHER for the first time when I was six. Though we shared the same blood, we looked nothing alike – him with his olive skin tone, dark eyes and hair – me, red-haired and pale, with freckles, my Irish side showing through. My recollection of the meeting is murky: Did we hug? Shake hands? Did he ask awkward questions such as "Well, aren't you a big boy?" or "Where'd you get that red hair?"

Was I loquacious in my answers, or mono-syllabic? I honestly don't remember. Why would I? He and I were complete strangers, after all, and I wasn't to see him again for another seven years.

Yet, I am upholstered with memories of my grandparents.

For two years, while my father was in the armed services, my mother lived with the Strother family. Following my birth and then my parents' divorce, she returned to her mother and father's house. But the Strothers were tenacious and immediately moved to within a block of the Kelly family stronghold.

So, even though I grew up without a father, I never suffered for it. Rather, my childhood was centered between two doting and protective families. Their attention was like the heat of a summer afternoon, filled with orange and gold light, enveloping.

I vividly remember picking out Christmas trees with my grandfather Kelly. We moved slowly around the lot drinking in the heady aromas of spruce and pine.

"Flocked or not flocked?" he said, peering down at me through rimless eyeglasses from under his cocked felt fedora.

"Flocked, Granddaddy, please can we get the flocked one?"

We loaded the tree into his 1947 Chevrolet station wagon and took it home. It must've taken hours to clean all the flocking out of the car, but he never complained. Not even when I had an emergency as he was driving me to first grade, and had to pee in the Chevy's floorboard. We called the car Old Huldy. Some things you never forget.

Then there was my grand-mother Strother. On summer evenings, she'd play the ukulele while sitting on the front porch and sing "Red Sails in the Sunset." When she bent

over the instrument, a hank of her jet-black hair would fall down over one eye. Between verses she'd blow it back using the corner of her mouth.

A big fan of rhythm and blues and early rock 'n roll, she some-times let me stay up late at night listening to the radio. I was nine when she took me to my first rock concert: Big Joe Turner, the Ink Spots, Bill Haley and the Comets and more. We sat in the balcony because the main floor was black seating only.

Photo by Barbara V. Evers

Pop — my father's father — worked for the Southern Railway, and sometimes let me tag along on his trips. In Memphis we stayed in a moldy-smelling old hotel frequented by railroaders, ate every meal out, and saw *Love Me Tender* twice. Back in Chattanooga, he took me to see Jerry Lee Lewis live and in person at the Memorial Auditorium. I believe he enjoyed the event every bit as much as I did. As we fought our way through the jostling after-show crowd, he grinned from ear to ear and said, "Now *that* was a sight to think about." It's one of my favorite expressions to this day.

My grandmother Kelly was a woman before her time, espousing racial harmony and acceptance long before civil rights became newsworthy. She was the arbiter of family arguments, the preparer of family feasts, and the *de facto* therapist for all family tragedies, big and small. As a young man, I borrowed six hundred dollars from her to deal with a medical emergency.

"I'll pay you back," I promised.

She gave me a loving and gracious smile. "I know you will."

I never got around to paying that money back, and she never once asked about it. It was our little secret, and she took it with her to the grave.

My head and heart are packed full of these, and hundreds more, warm, funny and exquisite recollections of my grandparents. So full I want my own grandchildren to know their great-great grandparents as I do. It's one of the reasons I write.

Even more, I want my grandchildren to grow into adulthood with those same kinds of memories of their grandparents. Perhaps it's wrong to want something so much. But I had no father in my life. My grandparents were my default family.

Fortunately, my grandchildren's families are intact. They have loving mothers and fathers who engage and embrace them every single day. These are the loving parents we have encouraged to build their own lives, and they've done what we envisioned for them: flown high and far and wide.

And they've taken my grandchildren with them.

Two in Arizona and two in West Virginia, they range in age from ten to five. There's Brody, the oldest, charming and competitive; Owen, who's six, a sensitive and artistic boy; Harper, five, who is absolutely fearless and sports a Cindy Lauper sense of fashion; and Darby, also five, who's both clever and innocently manipulative.

Whereas I spent most of my youth living within a city block of two sets of adoring grandparents, I now must travel hundreds or thousands of miles to spend limited amounts of time with my own grandkids. If I'm lucky, I will still be able to experience a few of their precious childhood moments, if not in person, at least digitally. Because it's what I have, I revel in it.

But will they remember me?

I tell myself I want to provide for them the same wondrous childhood I had. I suppose we all believe lies that bring us more comfort than the truth. What I truly want is to be remembered in the same way, with the same warmth and affection I have for my long-deceased grandparents— for my grandchildren to feel what I felt then and what I feel now. Proximity and familiarity is the key to that, but geography is a difficult adversary to overcome.

I watch the videos and look at photos I'm provided (along with countless other "friends") on Facebook: my Arizona brood skiing down Snowbowl or mountain biking together in the red rock canyons of Sedona; or the West Virginians huddled together playing video games in their living

Photo from Pixabay - CCO Public Domain

room and careening down the world's longest backyard Slip 'n Slide. And I'm forced to think that I'm perhaps viewing their lives from a skewed perspective. Maybe my grandkids *already* feel enveloped in the same warm cloak of love and family I experienced as a youth. Maybe they already have it all.

And their fathers, too.

Photo by Edith Hawkins

Contributors

Photo by Edith Hawkins

JENNIFER BARTELL, an English teacher at Spring Valley High School in Columbia, SC, graduated from Agnes Scott College in 2005 and received the MFA in Poetry from the University of South Carolina in 2014. Her poetry has been published in pluck!: *The Journal of Affrilachian Arts & Culture*, Blackberry: a magazine, *Jasper Magazine*, *decomP*, *Fall Lines*, and *Composite* {Arts Magazine} and is forthcoming in *Callaloo*. Jennifer is an administrator for *The Watering Hole*, a poetry collective for Southern poets and poets of color who write about the South. Jennifer is a 2014 *Callaloo* Writing Workshop Fellow.

JAYNE PADGETT BOWERS, a semi-retired educator, has published articles in *Guideposts*, *The Petigru Review*, and two LDS magazines, the *Ensign* and the *Liahona*. She is the author of *Human Relations in Industry* (Jayne Crolley), *Musings of a Missionary Mom*, *Eve's Sisters*, and *Crossing the Bridge: Succeeding in a Community College and Beyond*. Jayne contributed to the Camden Chapter's recent anthology, *Serving Up Memory*.

Find Jayne at JayneBowers.com.

LEAH BROWN is a freelance writer with a degree in English from USCA. She is involved in a variety of community volunteer projects while pursuing my creative writing proclivities. At first she focused on fiction and nonfiction, but in the past two years, poetry has become her main form of literary expression.

BARBARA V. EVERS works as a professional trainer and public speaker. She holds an MA in Professional Communication and is a Certified MBTI Instructor. Barbara's short stories and essays appear in *Child of My Child*, *The Petigru Review*, the *moonShine review*, and *Stupefying Stories*. She contributes regularly to five blogs, two of which are her own personal sites. She is an active member of South Carolina Writers' Workshop where she served three years on the board and now leads a local chapter.

DAVID DIXON is a father of two and currently lives in Mauldin. He attended the United States Military Academy at West Point and spent almost nine years as an active duty Army officer. During that time, he was deployed three times to Iraq, including one year where he lived and worked with the Iraqi Army as an advisor. Much of what he writes is informed by his experiences in Iraq.

M.B. GIBSON moved from her native New Jersey to Barnwell, SC, in 1977 where she taught middle school and raised a family. Retired, she writes historical fiction as well as children's stories. She was the 2012 Carrie McCray Award winner for First Chapter of a Novel and nominated for a Pushcart Prize. She was also a finalist in the 2013 Pacific Northwest Writers Association Contest in the historical fiction category. She has been published in *The Petigru Review*, *Nights of Horseplay*, and *Pockets* magazine.

ELAINE HOLLIDAY grew up in Spartanburg, SC. She majored in Creative Writing at Agnes Scott College, was published in Aurora, her college's literary magazine. She was a finalist in the Agnes Scott College Writer's Festival. She works as librarian and lives in Myrtle Beach with her husband and too many cats.

LEN LAWSON teaches writing at Morris College in Sumter, SC, where he was named 2013 Professor of the Year. His first book of poetry *The Very Least of Me* was an Amazon Kindle Best Seller in 2014. Len is a 2015 Berfrois Poetry Prize finalist with poems appearing in *Diverse Voices Quarterly, Pamplemousse, Control, Jasper,* and others.

KATHRYN Etters Lovatt is former winner of the Doris Betts Prize, she also won *Press* 53's short fiction competition in 2012 and in 2013. She won Carrie McCray Awards for short story and first chapter of a novel. Both her fiction and poetry have been nominated for Pushcart prizes. A Virginia Center for the Arts fellow, she received SC Art Commission's Individual Artist Fellowship for prose in 2013. Most recently, her work has appeared in *Serving up Memory,* an anthology written and published by SCWW, Camden Chapter. Her story, "Eminent Domain" will be published in NC Literary Review.

MICHAEL HUGH LYTHGOE has been nominated three times for a Pushcart prize. He is the author of *Holy Week* poems & *BRASS,* a chapbook. Mike is a contributor to *Rockburst Review, Kakalak, Windhover, Innisfree, Spillway, Christianity & Lit, Caribe Writer, Cairn* and *SIXFOLD*. He has won a literary prize from the Porter Fleming Foundation for nonfiction.

VALERIE KEISER NORRIS moved south 28 years ago with her husband and three daughters. She won the 2013 Hub City/EMRYS Creative Writing prize, the 2009 Carrie McCray fiction contest and Honorable Mention twice in *Writer's Digest* Fiction Competitions. Several stories have appeared in anthologies (*Sweeter*  *Than Tea* and *A Stone Mountain Christmas*). A novel excerpt, "Satan's Lingerie," won an award and was published in *The Petigru Review*, but somehow hasn't resulted in a book publishing contract. She's had short stories, articles and humor published in small magazines and occasionally posts to a humorous blog at ValerieNorris.blogspot.com.

CAROL-ANN RUDY, originally from British Columbia, Canada, was the writer for *The Miami Herald / el Nuevo Herald* Newspaper-In-Education chapter. She created a series of Character Education stories with supporting materials featured in a number of newspapers across the country. Currently, she has completed a Young Adult  coming-of-age novel and several Early Reader stories, and is working on a Young Adult dystopian, speculative novel. She is also a poet, an artist, and has performed and sung in Little Theatre performances. She and her husband make their home by a lake in Upstate South Carolina.

BOB STROTHER'S work has been published widely and internationally. His short story "Doughnut Walk"— originally published in the 2011 Petigru *Review* — was recently adapted for film. Previous publications include a short story collection, *Scattered, Smothered, and Covered* and a novel-in-stories, *Shug's Place*. His latest novel,  *Burning Time*, was released in July of this year. Strother is also a contributing writer for *Southern Writers Magazine*. He lives with his wife, Vicki, in Greenville, SC.

M.Z. THWAITE is the author of a literary suspense novel *Tidewater Rip*. A licensed Realtor and a native of Georgia, she writes and lives in Beaufort, SC, with her artist husband, Steve Weeks of Riverton, NJ.

FERGUSON WILLIAMS is currently working on her debut collection of short stories titled *Kush, Cognac, and Cigarettes*. Possessing a wicked imagination and a love of the English language, writing has always been her destiny. She currently resides in Socastee, SC, with her three most important possessions: her two children and her lap top.

DONNA WYLIE is a native of Charlotte, NC, who now makes her home in Rock Hill, SC. Donna has been an active member of SCWW since 2001. Her poems have been published in *Horizons, Carolina Nickel, Catfish Stew, The Petigru Review* and *Threads*, the Arts Council of York County's 2014 Annual Literary Competition Magazine. She has taken leadership roles in the Rock Hill chapter of SCWW and the Rock Hill Luncheon Literary Society. Donna is active on the Publicity Committee in promoting the 2015 SC Writers Intensive Workshop in Rock Hill. Donna is currently working on a book called *Dark Corner of War*.

Photographers

 Jayne Bowers

 Valerie Keiser Norris

 Barbara V. Evers

 Irena Tervo

 Edith Hawkins

 M.Z. Thwaite

 Michael Hugh Lythgoe

TPR

Judges

Photo by Edith Hawkins

POETRY

Lilah Hegnauer

LILAH HEGNAUER lives in Cambridge, MA, where she teaches online creative writing workshops for the University of Virginia. She was the 2013-2014 Amy Clampitt Poet in Residence in Lenox, MA. She has also taught poetry workshops and American Literature at Sweet Briar College, James Madison University, and the UVA Young Writers Workshop. Her second book of poetry, *Pantry*, won the Hub City Press

Photo by HR Hegnauer

New Southern Voices Poetry Award selected by D.A. Powell, and was published in February, 2014. She is also the author of *Dark Under Kiganda Stars* (Ausable Press 2005).

POETRY

Malaika Favorite

MALAIKA FAVORITE is a visual artist and writer. Poetry publications: *Dreaming at the Manor*, Finishing Line Press 2014, and *Illuminated Manuscript*,
by New Orleans Poetry Journal Press, 1991. Her
poetry, fiction and articles have appeared in numerous anthologies and journals including: *you say. say*
and *Hell strung and crooked* (Uphook Press), *Pen International, Hurricane Blues, Drumvoices review, Uncommon
Place, Xavier Review, The Maple Leaf Rag, Visions International, Louisiana Literature, Louisiana English Journal, Big Muddy,* and *Art Papers.* Also, *Down to the
Dark River, Contemporary poems about the Mississippi River;* editors: Philip C.
Kolin & Jack B. Bedell, Louisiana Literature Press, 2016. Favorite won the
Broadside Lotus Press Naomi Long Madgett Poetry Award for her collec-
tion of poems, *Ascension,* to be published by, Broadside Lotus Press, 2016.

"Read your work several times and remove
unnecessary words. Allow magic but erase
cliches. A good poem is a fresh arrangement
of old words.

FICTION

Jason Ockert

JASON OCKERT is the author of *Wasp Box*, his debut novel, and two collections of short stories: *Neighbors of Nothing* and *Rabbit Punches*. Winner of the Dzanc Short Story Collection Contest, the *Atlantic Monthly* Fiction Contest and the Mary Roberts Rinehart Award, he was also a finalist for the Shirley Jackson Award and the Million Writers Award. His work has appeared in journals and anthologies including *New Stories from the South*, *Best American Mystery Stories*, *Oxford American*, *The Iowa Review*, *One Story*, and *McSweeney's*. He teaches writing at Coastal Carolina University.

It was a great joy reading these stories. They indicate to me that the literary pulse is thrumming strong in South Carolina.

FICTION

Cary Holladay

CARY HOLLADAY'S seven volumes of fiction include *Horse People: Stories* (Louisiana State UP) and *The Deer in the Mirror* (Ohio State UP). She has received an O. Henry Prize and fellowships from the Pennsylvania Council on the Arts, the Tennessee Arts Commission and the National Endowment for the Arts. A native of Virginia, she teaches at the University of Memphis.

NONFICTION

Jim Minick

JIM MINICK is the author of four books, including *The Blueberry Years*, a memoir that won the Best Nonfiction Book of the Year from Southern Independent Booksellers Association. He has been awarded numerous honors, most recently the 2015 Jean Ritchie Fellowship in Appalachian Writing from Lincoln Memorial University, and the Fred Chappell Fellowship at University of North Carolina-Greensboro. His work has appeared in many publications including *Oxford American, Shenandoah, Orion, San Francisco Chronicle, Encyclopedia of Appalachia, Conversations with Wendell Berry, Appalachian Journal,* and *The Sun.*

Currently, he is Assistant Professor at Georgia Regents University and Core Faculty in Converse College's low-residency MFA program.

"Writers usually work in isolation, but we also belong to a large community of other writers and readers. To participate in this community—through judging a contest or writing a review or teaching a workshop or in many other ways—is always an honor, especially so in this case. *The Petigru Review* is a great journal and I'm glad to be part of the community it nourishes.

NONFICTION

Virginia Holman

VIRGINIA HOLMAN is the author of *Rescuing Patty Hearst* (Simon & Schuster), a memoir of her mother's untreated schizophrenia. It was a Barnes & Noble Discover Great New Authors Selection, and received the Outstanding Literature Award from the National Alliance on Mental Illness. She's published essays and articles in *DoubleTake Magazine, Redbook, Women's Health, Prevention, Glamour, Self, O Magazine, More*, the *Washington Post*, the *Atlanta Journal-Constitution*, and elsewhere. Her work has been reprinted in Pushcart Prize series, broadcast on *This American Life*, and she's received fellowships and awards from the North Carolina Arts Council and The Carter Center. An avid kayaker and outdoorsy type, she also writes the monthly "Excursions" column for *Salt Magazine* in Wilmington. She teaches at the University of North Carolina at Wilmington.

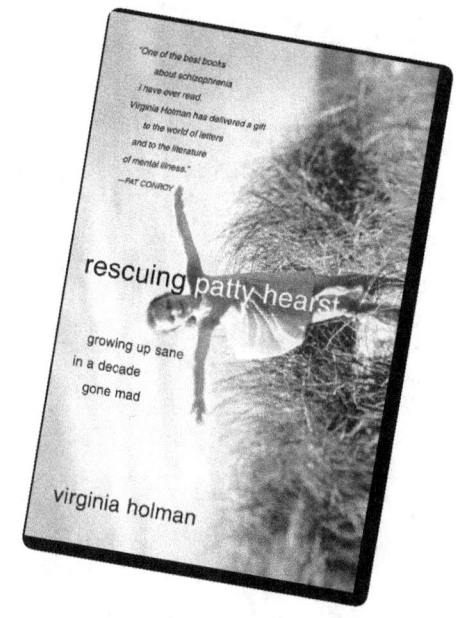

www.ingramcontent.com/pod-product-compliance
Lightning Source LLC
Chambersburg PA
CBHW071254130626
46556CB00003B/1315